# NARRATIVE STRATEGIES

## CONTENTS

| | |
|---|---|
| Introduction | 3 |
| The Well-Worn Muse: Adaptation in Film History and Theory — Dudley Andrew | 9 |
| Borges, Bertolucci, and Metafiction — Ulrich Wicks | 19 |
| Strick's Adaptation of Joyce's *Portrait of the Artist:* Discourse and Containing Discourse — Michael Klein | 37 |
| Narrative Discourse in Film and Fiction: The Question of the Present Tense — Joan Dagle | 47 |
| Audience Engagement in Wenders' *The American Friend* and Fassbinder's *Ali: Fear Eats the Soul* — Peter Ruppert | 61 |
| Mediation, the Novelistic, and Film Narrative — Judith Mayne | 79 |
| Tradition and the Individual Talent: Poetry in the Genre Film — Barry K. Grant | 93 |
| Ritual Patterns in Western Film and Fiction — Robert T. Self | 105 |
| Story, Pleasure, and Meaning in *The Scarlet Empress* — William Cadbury | 115 |
| Point of View and Narrative Voice in *The Grapes of Wrath:* Steinbeck and Ford — Doug Emory | 129 |
| Notes on Contributors | 137 |
| Editors' Note | 139 |

Copyright©1980 by Western Illinois University
Library of Congress Card No. 80-53296
ISBN 0-934312-03-6

**TO OUR PARENTS**

# Introduction

The extensive endnotes to many of the essays included in this anthology serve as an appropriate reminder that the question of comparable narrative strategies in film and fiction is by no means an entirely new one. A perusal of the articles, however, suggests how much is yet to be explored. Though the issues raised by our contributors are to some extent familiar ones—questions of tense, point of view, self-reflexivity, and audience response, for example—the authors addressing them review earlier assumptions and conclusions in order to present new perspectives. Ideas formulated by recent theorists such as Barthes, Iser, Lévi-Strauss, and Metz inform many of these discussions; they lead our writers to consider alternative directions for the discussion of film and prose fiction.

Dudley Andrew, in his introductory essay, has taken the lead in delineating profitable new areas for film and fiction research. Beginning with a traditional but narrow idea of adaptation, one that prescribes fidelity as the overriding criterion for successful transformations of fiction into film, Andrew broadens this concept significantly. He suggests that every motion picture is dependent upon preexisting material and, therefore, is an adaptation. Subsequently, however, he limits his discussion to books and films that foreground the relation between literary and cinematic texts. He presents three modes that define this relation: borrowing, intersection, and fidelity of transformation, and, after briefly describing the first two, explicates the third at greater length. He takes his discussion out of the realm of prescription and mechanical emulation to that of equivalencies between signifying systems. He shows how literature and cinema, on the level of narrative, are comparable; how because of shared narrative codes, they both operate on the level of connotation; and how, at this level, they must be analyzed in terms "of use as well as of system," that is, in terms of "artistic history, practice, and discourse" as well as of word and image systems. To illustrate the potential of this shift in emphasis, Andrew reviews the mutual stylistic influence of literature and film at various times, singling out naturalism to demonstrate how this influence is evident in a specific play and film (Gorki's and Renoir's *The Lower Depths*) as well as in groups of literary and cinematic works.

In the process of defining his own position, Andrew challenges earlier concepts, but his primary emphasis is on redefining adaptation and opening new areas for research and discussion. He insists that to make such study useful it is necessary to avoid a priori judgments and to be sensitive to the texts themselves. Our other contributors respond to the need for a reassessment in a variety of ways. Joan Dagle, Peter Ruppert, Barry K. Grant, and Doug Emory review commonly held notions about how cinematic and literary narratives work. They depend on recent linguistic, phenomenological, and structuralist theory to do so. Ulrich Wicks, Michael Klein, and Judith Mayne provide, not direct reevaluations, but explorations of newly formulated or reformulated areas of study, those of metafiction, lyrical narrative, and mediation. William Cadbury and Robert T. Self examine story lines and resolutions, Cadbury through the explication of a single film, Self through study of an evolving genre. Though the range of the essays is broad and the methodologies varied, each writer depends on individual literary and cinematic texts to attest to his or her assertions and each, in contrast to early concepts about film and fiction, assumes or stresses on the level of narrative discourse similarity rather than difference in film and prose fiction.

In "Borges, Bertolucci, and Metafiction," Wicks places the Borges tales "Theme of the Traitor" and the "Hero" and Bertolucci's film adaptation, *The Spider's Stratagem*, in the context of metafiction. A brief discussion of a few key novels and films in this tradition enables Wicks to distinguish between orthodox reflexivity and contemporary or modernist reflexivity and also provides him with a background against which to analyze the Borges and Bertolucci texts. His investigation contains a number of provocative assertions: 1) that Borges and Bertolucci manage to convey the same distrust of illusion even though their narratives are remarkably different in what are often assumed to be the most fundamental ingredients of a story; 2) that Bertolucci articulates this concern on the discursive level of the narrative (in the text of Borges, the level at which the narrator intrudes), the level Barthes has identified as " 'least transferable from novel to film' "; 3) that the tales of Borges and Bertolucci only seem to deprive us of illusion and disturb our faith in it; actually, they challenge only conventional kinds of illusion-making.

Klein is also concerned with self-reflection and the discursive level of narrative, but his study of Strick's adaptation of Joyce's *A Portrait of the Artist* leads him to draw conclusions quite distinct from Wicks's. Strick, Klein believes, is typical of a number of modern storytellers who resist making fictions that are merely self-reflective and who insist instead upon the importance of such traditional narrative values as mimesis and illusion. To achieve this, they strive to attain a point of view as close as possible to the camera's "which disinterestedly records both background and foreground simultaneously," a narrative perspective that Klein believes bears a resemblance to that of the self-effacing author. This camera vision does not negate subjective experience in the foreground but places it in a cultural context; it offers the viewer two discourses: one of the story's central consciousness, another of the "containing discourse" of the external world. Klein's essay, which also touches on the films of Kubrick and Olmi and the novels of Dos Passos, demonstrates that studying the constantly shifting balance between discourse and containing discourse can be a useful approach to narrative adaptations in both the narrower and the broader senses which

Andrew has given the term.

If Klein's essay increases awareness of film narrative's potentialities through the simultaneous presentation of both foreground and background, Dagle increases awareness of its potentialities for presenting past, present, and future. Dagle repudiates the critical maxim that films can only speak in the present tense. First she scrutinizes, one by one, a few of the unquestioned assumptions about film narrative that the maxim rests on: the irretrievability of the image viewed, dependence on projection time, the " 'presentness' " (Robbe-Grillet's assertion) of the film image. Then she offers a counter theory that stresses similarities between film and literary narratives: we have overlooked the possibility that film narratives contain tense signifiers, just as written narratives do; we fail to acknowledge these signifiers as critics (though perhaps not as viewers) because the images beyond them appear to be in the present tense. Dagle cites examples from the films of Godard, Welles, Truffaut, and Resnais, to support her hypothesis.

Ruppert reexamines another some time principle among comparatists of film and literature: that film, unlike literature, offers its viewers a passive, nonconceptual experience. Drawing on the reader-oriented narrative theories of Wolfgang Iser and Robert Scholes, Ruppert analyzes two recent films, Wim Wenders' *The American Friend* and R. W. Fassbinder's *Ali: Fear Eats the Soul*, to demonstrate that film narratives can be conceptually demanding. Wenders' film compels his viewers to participate in the creation of meaning, for example, to a much greater extent than does the author of the tale on which he bases his film. He does so by building into his text significant gaps or blanks in structure (negations of what the viewer expects to happen). Though Fassbinder's structure is more traditional, he, too, invites viewer participation by building gaps into the content of his film text (negations of what the viewer sees as normal or valuable). Through these strategies, which Ruppert believes bear some resemblance to Bertolt Brecht's famous *Verfremdungseffekt*, Wenders and Fassbinder present their viewers with an existential perception of the world (as ambiguous and anxiety producing) designed to shatter complacency.

Mayne's essay offers a compatible historical framework in which to place Ruppert's study of recent narratives which stimulate readers or viewers to create their own meanings. Mayne explores traditional narrative film and its literary ancestor, the classic novel, and finds that each controls rather than liberates its audience. Such narratives, with their seductive surface verisimilitude, have mediated not only deceptive information and vicarious pleasure to their audiences but also reinforced oppressive bourgeois structures and values. Women in the eighteenth and nineteenth centuries and urban workers in the twentieth century have been similarly exploited. They have been offered the consoling illusion of full participation in a just society although they were usually on the periphery of that society and it was often far from utopian. Mayne believes that modern narratives should move towards Barthes' ideal of the writerly text, the text which allows for maximum reader/viewer involvement.

Grant and Self, like Ruppert and Mayne, are interested in how film and literature are received by—and may also reflect the views of—readers and spectators. Grant's inquiry leads him to a consideration of cinematic poetry and genre films. He challenges assertions that the specificity of visual images precludes cinematic poetry and he refutes critics who suggest that poetic cinema can be defined in terms of parallels between metaphor and montage, simply in terms of the degree and kind of audience response, or in terms of opposition between lyric and narrative films. Studying the movies of directors who are referred to as poets (he chooses D. W. Griffith and John Ford) and adopting Ezra Pound's description of written poetry—"the most concentrated form of verbal [visual, cinematographic] expression"—as a definition of film poetry, Grant concludes that the films most readily identified with the poetic are genre movies. Their poetic quality arises from the layers of meaning gradually revealed in their iconography and conventions, their codification of social beliefs and values, and their capacity to express the cultural myths of their audiences.

Grant opens the way to further discussion of poetry in prose narrative, implying that, on the level of generic discourse, film and fiction share certain dimensions. Self also focuses on questions of genre. He moves away from distinctions between visual and written narration to study a single genre, the western. Recognized as central to this discussion are the complexity and ambiguity of the wilderness versus civilization paradigm, the pivotal conflict around which ritualistic narrative structures of the western revolve. Citing western fiction by Twain, Guthrie, Crane, and Berger, along with western films directed by Wyler, Zinnemann, Ford, Altman and Penn, Self explores the manipulation of these structures in traditional, parodic, and formally self-conscious narratives. He shows how these reflect contemporary thought while unfolding the drama of the past and he discusses their relation to ambiguity, artistic quality, and audience sophistication.

Cadbury and Emory bring readers back to a consideration of individual films. In his interpretation of Josef von Sternberg's *The Scarlet Empress,* Cadbury demonstrates the significance of chronology and of story, and Emory, using John Ford's *The Grapes of Wrath* to support his contentions, argues for recognition of film's ability to convey multiple points of view. Cadbury explicitly questions the critical stance Laura Mulvey takes in her well-known 1975 *Screen* article, "Visual Pleasure and Narrative Cinema," and Robin Wood's reading of the von Sternberg film as explicated in "The Play of Light and Shadow: *The Scarlet Empress,*" an essay first published in *Film Comment* in 1975. Cadbury asserts that while Wood's descriptive analysis emphasizing imagery and motifs is incomplete and leads to a misinterpretation of character and motivation, Mulvey's concentration on the visual, generally erotic, pleasure evoked by the Dietrich image leads her to ignore other legitimate pleasures, including the intellectual pleasure of film viewing. Stressing the progression and interrelatedness of the events that affect Dietrich's Catherine, Cadbury insists that our understanding of the character is dependent upon such a systematic reading since Catherine's story is one of growth and increasing awareness.

Reacting to a tendency by some film critics to characterize film as impersonal and objective because of the camera's capacity to record external phenomena and events, Emory suggests that film can and does go beyond the objective third-person narration it has been identified with to convey subjective points of view. Through close analysis of specific sequences in *Grapes of Wrath,* Emory shows how Ford subtly utilizes visual and aural motifs as well as subjective camera shots to shift between first- and third-person narration. This enables Ford to project an empathy with the Okies similar to that John Steinbeck revealed in the more overt political and social commentary he interspersed with his dramatic presentation of the Joad family. Implicit in each of the essays, finally, is our own conviction that critics have just begun to investigate many questions about the nature of narrative. If our anthology stimulates further inquiry and discussion on just a few of those questions, then it has served its intended purpose.

*S.M.C. and J.R.W.*

# The Well-Worn Muse:
# Adaptation in Film History and Theory

### DUDLEY ANDREW

Frequently the most narrow and provincial area of film theory, discourse about adaptation is potentially as far reaching as you like. Its distinctive feature, the matching of the cinematic sign system to a prior achievement in some other system, can be shown to be distinctive of all representational cinema.

Let us begin with an example, *A Day in the Country*. Jean Renoir set himself the task of putting his knowledge, his troupe, and his artistry at the service of a tale by Guy de Maupassant. No matter how we judge the process or success of the film, its being owes something to the tale which was its inspiration and potentially its measure. That tale, "A Country Excursion," bears a transcendent relation to any and all films which adapt it, for it is itself an artistic sign with a given shape and value if not a finished meaning. A new artistic sign will then feature this original sign as either its signified or its referent. Adaptations claiming fidelity bear the original as a signified, while those which are inspired by or derived from an earlier text stand in a relation of referring to the original.

The notion of a transcendent order to which the system of the cinema is beholden in its practice goes well beyond this limited case of adaptation.[1] What is a city symphony, for example, if not an adaptation of a concept by the cinema.[2] A definite notion of Berlin preexisted Walter Ruttman's 1927 treatment of that city. What is any documentary, for that matter, except the signification by the cinema of some prior whole, some concept of person, place, event, or situation. If we take seriously the arguments of marxist and other social theorists that our consciousness is not open to the world but filters the world according to the shape of its ideology, then every cinematic rendering will exist in relation to some prior whole lodged unquestioned in the personal or public system of experience. In other words, no filmmaker (at least none working in the representational mode) responds immediately to reality itself, or to his own inner vision. Every representational film adapts a prior conception. Indeed the very term "representation" suggests the existence of a model. Adaptation delimits representation by insisting on the cultural status of the model, on its existence in the mode of the text or the already textualized. In the case of those texts which are explicitly termed "adaptations," the cultural model which the cinema represents is already treasured as a representation in another sign system.

This broader notion of the process of adaptation has much in common with interpretation theory, for in a strong sense adaptation is the appropriation of a meaning from a prior text. The hermeneutic circle, central to interpretation theory, preaches that an explication of a text occurs only after a prior understanding of it, yet that prior understanding is justified by the careful explication it allows.[3] In other words, before we can go about discussing and analyzing a text we must have a global conception of its meaning. Adaptation is similarly both a leap and a process. It can put into play the intricate mechanism of its signifiers only in response to a general understanding of the signified it aspires to have constructed at the end of its process. While all representational films function this way (as interpretations of a person, place, situation, event), we reserve a special place for those films which foreground this relation by announcing themselves as versions of some standard whole. A standard whole can only be a text. A version of it is an adaptation in the narrow sense.

While these speculations so far encourage a hopelessly broad view of adaptation, there is no question that the restricted view of adaptation from known texts in other art forms offers a privileged locus for analysis. I do not say that such texts are themselves privileged. Indeed the thrust of my earlier remarks suggests quite the opposite. Nevertheless the explicit, foregrounded relation of a cinematic text to a well-constructed original text which it derives from and in some sense strives to reconstruct provides the analyst with a clear and useful laboratory condition which he neglects only to his own detriment.

The making of a film out of an earlier text is virtually as old as the machinery of cinema itself. Well over half of all commercial films have come from literary originals, though by no means all of these originals are revered or respected. If we confine ourselves to those cases where the adaptation process is foregrounded, that is, where the original is held up as a worthy source or goal, there are still several modes of relation between the film and the text which may obtain. These modes can, for convenience, be reduced to three: borrowing, intersection, and fidelity of transformation.

In the history of the arts, surely borrowing names the most frequent mode of adaptation. Here the artist employs, more or less extensively, the material, idea, or form of an earlier, generally successful text. Medieval paintings featuring biblical iconography and miracle plays based on Bible stories draw on an exceptional text whose power they borrow. In a later, secular age the artworks of an earlier generation might be used as sacred in their own right. The many adaptations of Shakespeare's plays come readily to mind. Doubtless in these cases the adapting artists hope to win an audience by the prestige of their borrowed titles or subjects. At the same time they seek to gain a certain respectability, if not aesthetic value, as a dividend in the transaction. Adaptations from literature to music, opera, or paintings are of this nature. There is no question of the replication of the original in Richard Strauss's *Don Quixote*. Instead the audience is expected to enjoy basking in a certain preestablished presence and to call up new or especially powerful aspects of a cherished work.

To study this mode of adaptation, the analyst needs to probe the source of power in the original by examining the use made of it in adaptation. Here the main concern is the generality of the original, its potential for wide and varied appeal; in short, its existence as a continuing form or archetype in culture. This is especially true of that adapted material which, because of its frequent reappearance, claims the status of myth: *Tristan and Isolde* for certain, *A Midsummer Night's Dream* possibly. The success of adaptations of this sort rests on the issue of their fertility not their fidelity. Frank McConnell's book, *Storytelling and Mythmaking*,[4] catalogues the garden of culture by examining borrowing as the history of grafting and transplantation in the fashion of Northrop Frye or even Carl G. Jung. This direction of study will always elevate film by demonstrating its participation in a cultural enterprise whose value is outside film and, for Jung and others, outside texts altogether. Adaptation is the name of this cultural venture at its most explicit, though McConnell, Frye, and Jung would all immediately want to extend their theories of artistic fertility to original texts which, upon inspection, show their dependence on the great fructifying symbols and mythic patterns of civilization.

This vast mode of adaptation as borrowing finds its opposite in that attitude toward adaptation I choose to call intersection. Here the uniqueness of the original text is preserved to such an extent that it is intentionally left unassimilated in adaptation. The cinema, as a separate mechanism, records its confrontation with an ultimately intransigent text. Undoubtedly the key film sponsoring this relation is Robert Bresson's *Diary of a Country Priest*. André Bazin, championing this film and this mode,[5] claimed that in this instance we are presented not with an adaptation so much as a refraction of the original. Because Bresson featured the writing of the diary and because he went out of his way to avoid opening up or in any other way cinematizing the original, Bazin claims that the film is the novel as seen by cinema. To extend one of his most elaborate metaphors,[6] the original artwork can be likened to a crystal chandelier whose formal beauty is a product of its intricate but fully artificial arrangement of parts while the cinema would be a crude flashlight interesting not for its own shape or the quality of its light but for what it makes appear in this or that dark corner. The intersection of Bresson's flashlight and the chandelier of Georges Bernanos's novel produces an experience of the original modulated by the cinema. Naturally a great deal of the Bernanos work fails to be lit up, but what is lit up is only that work as seen by the cinema.

The modern cinema is increasingly interested in just this sort of intersection. Bresson, naturally, has given us his Joan of Arc from court records and his *Mouchette,* once again from Bernanos. Jean-Marie Straub has filmed Pierre Corneille's *Othon* and *The Chronicle of Anna Magdalena Bach*. Pier Paolo Pasolini audaciously confronted Matthew's gospel with many later texts (musical, pictorial, and cinematic) which it inspired. His later *Medea, Canterbury Tales,* and *Decameron* are also adaptational events in the intersectional mode. In all such works, he fears or refuses to adapt. Instead he presents the otherness and distinctiveness of the original text, initiating a dialectical interplay between the aesthetic forms of one epoch with the cinematic forms of our own epoch. In direct contrast to the search for aesthetic generality by which scholars have treated the mode of borrowing, these intersections compel the analyst to attend to the specificity of the original within the specificity of the cinema. An original is allowed its life, its own life, in the cinema. The consequences of this method, despite its apparent forthrightness, are neither innocent nor simple. Indeed, the disjunct experience such intersection promotes is consonant with the aesthetics of modernism in all the arts. The existence of this mode calls into question the commonplace that adaptations support only a conservative film aesthetics.

Unquestionably the most frequent and most tiresome discussion of adaptation (and of film and literature relations as well) concerns fidelity and transformation. Here it is assumed that the task of adaptation is the reproduction in cinema of something essential about an original text; we have a clear-cut case of a film trying to measure up to a literary work, or of an audience expecting to make such a comparison. Fidelity of adaptation is conventionally treated in relation to the letter and to the spirit of the text, as though adaptation were the rendering of an interpretation of a legal precedent. The letter would appear to be within the reach of cinema for it can be emulated in mechanical fashion. It includes aspects of fiction generally elaborated in any film script: the characters and their inter-relation, the geographical, sociological, and cultural information providing the fiction's context, and the basic narrational aspects which determine the point of view of the narrator (tense, degree of participation, and knowledge of the storyteller, etc.). Ultimately, and this was Bazin's complaint about faithful transformations, the literary work can readily become a scenario written in typical scenario form. The skeleton of the original can, more or less thoroughly, become the skeleton of a film.

More difficult is fidelity to the spirit, to the original's tone, values, imagery, and rhythm, for finding stylistic equivalents in film for these intangible aspects is the opposite of a mechanical process. The cineaste presumably must intuit and reproduce the feeling of the original. It has been argued variously that this is frankly impossible, or that it involves the systematic replacement of verbal signifiers by cinematic signifiers, or that it is the product of artistic intuition, as when Bazin found the pervasive snowy decor in *Symphonie Pastorale* (1946) to reproduce adequately the simple past tense which André Gide's verbs all bear in that tale.[7]

It is at this point that the specificity of these two signifying systems is at stake. Generally film is found to work from perception toward signification, from external facts to interior motivations and consequences, from the givenness of a world to the meaning of a story cut out of that world. Literary fiction works oppositely. It begins with signs, graphemes and words, building to propositions which attempt to develop perception. As a product of human language it naturally treats human motivation and values, seeking to throw them out onto the external world, elaborating a world out of a story.

George Bluestone, Jean Mitry, and a host of others find this opposition to be most graphic in adaptations.[8] Therefore they take pleasure in scrutinizing this practice even while ultimately condemning it to the realm of the impossible. Since signs name the inviolate relation of signifier to signified, how is translation of poetic texts conceivable from one language to another (where signifiers belong to different systems); much less, how is it possible to transform the signifiers of one material (verbal) to signifiers of another material (images and sounds)? It would appear that one must presume the global signified of the original to be separable from its text if one believes it can be approximated by other sign clusters. Can we attempt to reproduce the meaning of the *Mona Lisa* in a poem, or of a poem in a musical phrase, or even of a musical phrase in an aroma? If one accepts this possibility at the very least one is forced to discount the primary articulations of the relevant language systems. One would have to hold that while the material of literature (graphemes, words, and sentences) may be of a different nature from the materials of cinema (projected light and shadows, identifiable sounds and forms, and represented actions), both systems may construct in their own way, and at a higher level, scenes and narratives which are indeed commensurable.

The strident and often futile arguments over these issues can be made sharper and more consequential in the language of E. H. Gombrich or the even more systematic language of semiotics. Gombrich finds that all discussion of adaptation introduces the category of "matching."[9] First of all, like Bazin he feels one cannot dismiss adaptation since it is a fact of human practice. We can and do correctly match items from different systems all the time: a tuba sound is more like a rock than like a piece of string; it is more like a bear than like a bird; more like a romanesque church than a baroque one. We are able to make these distinctions and insist on their public character because we are matching equivalents. In the system of musical instruments the tuba occupies an equivalent position to that enjoyed by the romanesque in its system of architectural styles. Nelson Goodman has treated this issue at length in *The Language of Art*[10] pointing to the equivalence not of elements but of the position elements occupy vis-à-vis their different domains. Names of properties of colors may thus metaphorically, but correctly, describe aspects of the world of sound (a blue note, a somber or bright tone). Adaptation would then become a matter of searching two systems of communication for elements of equivalent position in the systems capable of eliciting a signified at a given level of pertinence, for example, the description of a narrative action. For Gombrich adaptation is possible, though never perfect, because every artwork is a construct of elements built out of a traditional use of a system. Since humans have the general capacity to adapt to new systems with different traditions in achieving a like goal or construct, artistic adaptation poses no insurmountable obstacles. Nevertheless, attention to such "proportional consistencies" demands that the study of adaptation include the study of both art forms in their proper historic context.

Gombrich and Goodman anticipated the more fashionable vocabulary of semiotics in their clarification of these issues. In a recent book *Film and Fiction: The Dynamics of Exchange,* Keith Cohen tries to justify this new, nearly scientific approach to questions of relations between these arts. He writes, citing Christian Metz:

> A basic assumption I make is that both words and images are sets of signs that belong to systems and that, at a certain level of abstraction, these systems bear resemblances to one another. More specifically, within each such system there are many different codes (perceptual, referential, symbolic). What makes possible, then, a study of the relation between two separate sign systems, like novel and film, is the fact that the same codes may reappear in more than one

system .... The very mechanisms of language systems can thus be seen to carry on diverse and complex interrelations: "one function, among others, of language is to name the units segmented by vision (but also to help segment them), and ... one function, among others, of vision is to inspire semantic configurations (but also to be inspired by them)."[11]

Cohen, like Metz before him, suggests that despite their very different material character, despite even the different ways we process them at the primary level, verbal and cinematic signs share a common fate: that of being condemned to connotation. This is especially true in their fictional use where every signifier identifies a signified but also elicits a chain reaction of other relations which permits the elaboration of the fictional world. Thus, for example, imagery functions equivalently in films and novels. This mechanism of implication among signs leads Cohen to conclude that "narrativity is the most solid median link between novel and cinema, the most pervasive tendency of both verbal and visual languages. In both novel and cinema, groups of signs, be they literary or visual signs, are apprehended consecutively through time; and this consecutiveness gives rise to an unfolding structure, the diegetic whole that is never fully *present* in any one group yet always *implied* in each such group."[12]

Narrative codes, then, always function at the level of implication or connotation. Hence they are potentially comparable in a novel and a film. The story can be the same if the narrative units (characters, events, motivations, consequences, context, viewpoint, imagery) are produced equally in two works. Now this production is, by definition, a process of connotation and implication. The analysis of adaptation then must point to the achievement of equivalent narrative units in the absolutely different semiotic systems of film and language. Narrative itself is a semiotic system available to both and derivable from both. If a novel's story is judged in some way comparable to its film adaptation, then the strictly separate but equivalent processes of implication which produced the narrative units of that story respectively through words and audiovisual signs must be studied. Here semiotics coincides with Gombrich's intuition: such a study is not comparative between the arts but is instead intensive within each art. And since the implicative power of literary language and of cinematic signs is a function of use as well as of system, adaptation analysis ultimately leads to an investigation of film styles and periods in relation to literary styles of different periods.

We have come round the other side of the argument now to find once more that the study of adaptation is logically tantamount to the study of the cinema as a whole. The system by which film involves us in fictions and the history of that system are ultimately the questions we face even when starting with the simple observation of an equivalent tale told by novel and film. This is not to my mind a discouraging arrival for it drops adaptation and all studies of film and literature out of the realm of eternal principle and airy generalization, and onto the uneven but solid ground of artistic history, practice, and discourse.

It is time for adaptation studies to take a sociological turn. How does adaptation serve the cinema? What conditions exist in film style and film culture to warrant or demand the use of literary prototypes? While adaptation may be calculated as a relatively constant volume in the history of cinema, its particular function in any moment is far from constant. The choices of the mode of adaptation and of prototypes suggest a great deal about filmmakers' aspirations and sense of the role of cinema from decade to decade. Moreover, the stylistic strategies developed to achieve the proportional equivalences necessary to construct matching stories not only are symptomatic of a period's style but may crucially alter that style.

Bazin pointed to an important instance of this in the immediate postwar era[13] when adaptations from the stage by Jean Cocteau, Orson Welles, Laurence Olivier, William Wyler, and others not only developed new ways for the cinema to be adequate to serious theater, but also developed a kind of discipline in mise-en-scène whose consequences go far beyond the production of *Les Parents Terribles, Macbeth, Henry V,* and *The Little Foxes. Les Parents Terribles,* to take one example, derives its style from Welles's use of interior shooting in *Citizen Kane* and *The Magnificent Ambersons,* thus responding to a new conception of dramatic space; but at the same time Cocteau's film helped solidify a shooting style that would leave its mark on, among others, Alexandre Astruc and André Michel. Furthermore, his particular cinematic *écriture* would allow François Truffaut to set him against the cinema of quality in the famous 1954 diatribe.[14] It is instructive to note that while Truffaut railed against the status quo for its literariness and especially for its method of adaptation, the directors he praised were also working with literary originals: Bresson adapting Bernanos, Max Ophuls adapting Maupassant and Arthur Schnitzler, Cocteau adapting his own theater pieces. Like Bazin, Truffaut looked upon adaptation not as a monolithic practice to be avoided but as an instructive barometer for the age. The cinema *d'auteur* which he advocated was not to be pitted against a cinema of adaptation; rather one method of adaptation would be pitted against another. In this instance adaptation was the battleground even while it prepared the way for a stylistic revolution, the New Wave, which would for the most part avoid famous literary sources.

To take another sort of example, particular literary fashions have at times exercised enormous power over the cinema and, consequently, over the general direction of its stylistic evolution. The Romantic fiction of Victor Hugo, Charles Dickens, Alexandre Dumas, and countless lesser figures originally set the stylistic requirements of American and mainstream French cinema at the end of the silent era. Similarly Émile Zola and Maupassant, always of interest to French cineastes, helped Renoir muscularly reorient the style of world cinema in the 1930s. Not only that, Luchino Visconti developed this naturalist impulse directly into one strain of neorealism in his adaptations of Giovanni Verga (*La Terra Trema*) and James M. Cain (*Ossessione*).

This latter case forces us to recall that the "dynamics of exchange," as Cohen calls it, go both ways between film and fiction. Naturalist fiction helped cinema develop its interest in squalid subjects and a hard-hitting style. This in turn affected American hard-boiled novelists like Cain and Dashiell Hammett, eventually returning to France in the film style of Visconti, Marcel

Carné, Henri-Georges Clouzot, and others. This general trading between film and literature in the currency of naturalism had some remarkable individual incidents associated with it. Renoir's adaptation of *The Lower Depths* can serve as an example. In 1884 Zola had cried out for a naturalist theater[15] and had described twenty years before the time precisely the sort of drama Maxim Gorki would write in *The Lower Depths:* a collection of real types thrown together without a domineering plot, the drama driven by the natural rhythms of little incidents and facts exposing the general quality of life in an era. Naturalism here coincided with a political need, Gorki's play preceding the great uprisings in Russia by only a few years.

In another era and in response to a different political need, Renoir leapt at the chance to adapt the Gorki. This was 1935, the year of the ascendancy of the Popular Front and Renoir's treatment of the original is clearly marked by the pressures and aspirations of that moment. The film negotiates the mixture of classes which the play only hints at. Louis Jouvet as the Baron dominates the film, descending into the social depths and helping organize a collective undoing of Kostilev, the capitalist landlord. Despite the gloomy theme, the murder, jailing, deaths by sickness and suicide, Renoir's version overflows with a general warmth evident in the open setting by the Marne and the relaxed direction of actors who breathe languidly between their lines.

Did Gorki mind such an interpretation? We can never know, since he died a few months before its premiere. But he did give Renoir his imprimatur and looked forward to seeing the completed version, this despite the fact that in 1932 he declared that the play was useless, out of date, and unperformable in socialist Russia. Perhaps these statements were the insincere self-criticism which that important year elicited from many Russian artists. I prefer, however, to take Gorki at his word. More farsighted than most theorists, let alone authors, he realized that *The Lower Depths* in 1932 Russia was by no means the same artwork as *The Lower Depths* in the France of the Popular Front. This is why he put no strictures on Renoir assuming that the cineaste would deal with his play as he felt necessary. Necessity is, among other things, a product of the specific place and epoch of the adaptation, both historically and stylistically. The naturalist movement of 1904, fleshing out the original plans of Zola, gives way to a new historic and stylistic moment, and feeds that style which Renoir had begun elaborating ever since *La Chienne* in 1931, and which, despite its alleged looseness in comparison to the Gorki, would help lead European cinema into a period of naturalism.

This sketch of a few examples from the sociology of adaptation has rapidly taken us into the complex interchange among eras, styles, nations, and subjects. This is as it should be, for adaptation, while a tantalizing keyhole for theorists, nevertheless partakes of the universal situation of film practice, dependent as it is on the aesthetic system of the cinema in a particular era and on that era's cultural needs and pressures. Filmmaking, in other words, is always an event in which a system is used and altered in discourse. Adaptation is a peculiar form of discourse but not an unthinkable one. Let us use it not to fight battles over the essence of the media or the inviolability of individual art works. Let us use it as we use all cultural practices: to understand the world from which it comes and the one toward which it points. The elaboration of these worlds will demand, therefore, historical labor and critical acumen. The job of theory in all this is to keep the questions clear and in order. It will no longer do to let theorists settle things with a priori arguments. We need to study the films themselves as acts of discourse. We need to be sensitive to that discourse and to the forces that motivate it.

*University of Iowa*

## NOTES

[1] For this idea I am indebted to a paper written by Dana Benelli in a class at the University of Iowa, Autumn 1979.

[2] The "city symphony" is a genre of the 1920s which includes up to 15 films all built on formal or abstract principles, yet dedicated to the presentation of a single city, be it Berlin, Paris, Nice, or Moscow.

[3] In the theory of interpretation this is generally attributed to Dilthey, although Martin Heidegger has made much of it in our century.

[4] Frank McConnell, *Storytelling and Mythmaking: Images from Film and Literature* (New York: Oxford Univ. Press, 1979).

[5] André Bazin, *What is Cinema?* ed. and trans. by Hugh Gray (Berkeley: Univ. of California Press, 1967), p. 142.

[6] Bazin, p. 107.

[7] Bazin, p. 68.

[8] George Bluestone, *Novels into Film* (1957, rpt. Berkeley: Univ. of California Press, 1968), and Jean Mitry, "Remarks on the Problem of Cinematic Adaptation," *Bulletin of the Midwest Modern Language Association,* 10 (Spring 1971), 1-9.

[9] E. H. Gombrich, *Art and Illusion* (Princeton, N.J.: Princeton Univ. Press, 1960), p. 370.

[10] Nelson Goodman, *The Languages of Art* (Indianapolis, Ind.: Hackett, 1976), especially pp. 143-48.

[11] Keith Cohen, *Film and Literature: The Dynamics of Exchange* (New Haven, Conn.: Yale Univ. Press, 1979), pp. 3-4. Cohen's citation from Metz comes from Christian Metz, *Langage et Cinéma* (Paris: Larousse, 1971), p. 24.

[12] Cohen, p. 92.

[13] Bazin, p. 76.

[14] François Truffaut, "A Certain Tendency in French Cinema" (1954), rpt. in *Movies and Methods,* ed. Bill Nichols (Berkeley: Univ. of California Press, 1976), pp. 224-36.

[15] Émile Zola, "Naturalism and the Theater," in *The Experimental Novel and Other Essays,* trans. Belle M. Sherman (New York: Haskell House, 1964).

# Borges, Bertolucci, and Metafiction

## ULRICH WICKS

> Why does it disturb us that Don Quixote be a reader of the *Quixote* and Hamlet a spectator of *Hamlet*? I believe I have found the reason: these inversions suggest that if the characters of a fictional work can be readers or spectators, we, its readers or spectators, can be fictitious.
>
> Jorge Luis Borges, "Partial Magic in the *Quixote*"

If we want to give Borges' story "Theme of the Traitor and the Hero"[1] a literary ancestry (and progeny), we might find it in a tradition of which the following historical sequence of fictions can be representative: Cervantes' *Don Quixote* (1605, 1615), Sterne's *Tristram Shandy* (1760-67), Gide's *The Counterfeiters* (1925), and Barth's *Lost in the Funhouse* (1968). These are all self-conscious, self-reflexive fictions whose central concern—technically and thematically, discursively and diegetically—is fiction making itself. In Part I of *Don Quixote*, Cervantes gives us a prologue about not writing a prologue, a signal to us that the fiction that follows is going to be similarly self-reflexive. Early in Part I, Cervantes introduces Cide Hamete Benengeli, an Arab *historiador* whose fidelity to truth is often challenged (by the narrator, by the Moorish translator, and by Quixote himself) in the name of fiction; at one point he is called an Arab liar, and Don Quixote repeatedly confuses this historian with an enchanter, who transforms reality into illusion. Never do Don Quixote and Sancho Panza become aware of their book existence, but in Part II they become aware of the existence of a book about them. All of the events of Part II take place in a world which knows (and in which materially exists) Part I of the book we're reading. As characters, Don Quixote and Sancho Panza have their real existence to contend with, a book existence that coincides with their immediate real past, and another book existence (Avellaneda's false continuation) that grew out of the first book existence but not out of their real lives (there is also, of course, the book that Don Quixote imagines will be written about him, but it is always in the future tense, though his imaginings coexist with his adventures). In absorbing Part I into itself, Part II of *Don Quixote* becomes a fiction that destroys its illusions behind itself as it creates further illusions ahead, a double movement in which book and world contain each other. Toward the end, Don Quixote meets Don Alvaro Tarfe, a character from the false continuation, the reality of which Cervantes simultaneously acknowledges and destroys by bringing to life in his fictional world a character from it. Don Quixote, so often touted as the first novel, is also a paradigm of all fictions; it is exemplary of fiction making itself. Cervantes, as has been pointed out, "is the patron saint of metafiction."[2]

In *Tristram Shandy* we are presented with a self-conscious dramatized narrator for whom narrating time, because it flows on and accumulates, is never sufficient to contain narrated time; remembering takes up too much time itself, and so the remembered past is always incomplete. In Chapter 33 of Book VI Tristram loses himself and must begin the chapter over; in Chapter 39 of Book VI there is a blank page on which the reader can make his own contribution to the story; in Chapter 17 of Book IX, Tristram cannot narrate because his uncle, in a situation Tristram has just been rendering, is whistling a song. This one-to-one correspondence among content time, narrating time, and reading time leads us ultimately into the same perpetual and frustrating present we find in Robbe-Grillet's *The Voyeur* (1955), where the borderline between experiential reality and constructed fiction ceases to exist.

In Gide's *The Counterfeiters,* Edouard, a novelist, is writing a novel which will turn out to be the very book we are reading, though Gide is ostensibly narrating the reality of the actuality from which Edouard will create his fiction. The book's theme is that all perceptions of reality are counterfeit. Edouard writes in his journal, "I am beginning to catch sight of what I might call the 'deep-lying subject' of my book. It is—it will be—no doubt, the rivalry between the real world and the representation of it which we make to ourselves. The manner in which the world of appearances imposes itself upon us, and the manner in which we try to impose on the outside world our own interpretations—that is the drama of our lives."[3] One of the stories in Barth's *Lost in the Funhouse* is narrated by itself ("Autobiography: A Self-Recorded Fiction"); another, the title story, stops repeatedly while the narrator assesses the very story he is creating, constructing a narrating labyrinth that parallels the funhouse which is part of the story's substance; and yet another ("Life-Story") contains a deuteragonist who is you, the reader, in a story of infinite narrative regress: "Another story about a writer writing a story! Another regressus in infinitum! Who doesn't prefer art that at least overtly imitates something other than its own processes? That doesn't continually proclaim 'Don't forget I'm an artifice!'? That takes for granted its mimetic nature instead of asserting it in order (not so slyly after all) to deny it, or vice-versa?"[4] The labyrinths of Barth's funhouse of fiction are much like the "infinite book" Borges himself suggests in "The Garden of Forking Paths," a book "whose last page was identical with the first, a book which had the possibility of continuing indefinitely,"[5] a concept Barth has fun with in the Moebius strip fiction that begins *Lost in the Funhouse.*

These examples illustrate a broad tradition or context within which the Borges text works. Recently we have come to call such work "metafiction." In apparently coining the term, William Gass justifies it by saying that "everywhere lingos to converse about lingos are being contrived, and the case is no different in the novel," and defines it as that fiction in which "the forms of fiction serve as the material upon which further forms can be imposed"; moreover, it "is characteristic of this kind of writing to give overt expression to its nature, provide its own evaluation . . . ."[6] Roland Barthes, though he is including much more in his term, would call a metafictional text a "writerly" (*scriptible*) one, which we value today because "the goal of literary work (of literature as work) is to make the reader no longer a consumer, but a producer of the text." (The "readerly" text, in contrast, is "a classic text.") "The writerly text," Barthes goes on, "is a perpetual present upon which no *consequent* language (which would inevitably make it past) can be superimposed; the writerly text is *ourselves writing,* before the infinite play of the world (the world as function) is traversed, intersected, stopped, plasticized by some singular system (Ideology, Genus, Criticism) which reduces the plurality of entrances, the opening of networks, the infinity of languages."[7] Robert Scholes sees metafiction as assimilating "all the perspectives of criticism into the fictional process itself. It may emphasize structural, formal, behavioral, or philosophical qualities."[8] He works out a diagram of four basic fictional forms, which correspond to the four dimensions of criticism: 1) fiction of ideas (myth)–structural criticism; 2) fiction of forms (romance)–formal criticism; 3) fiction of existence (novel)–behavioral criticism; and 4) fiction of essence (allegory)–philosophical criticism. And Robert Alter, who got the title for his book-length study of metafiction from Borges, reminds us (as I have tried to do with the examples I began with) that metafiction is at least as old as that which we have come to call, generically, the novel. From its beginnings, the novel has explored itself self-reflexively. Though Alter avoids the term "metafiction" he might as well be describing it when he says: "Knowing that a fiction is, after all, only a fiction, is potentially subversive of any meaningful reality that might be attributed to the fiction, while assenting imaginatively to the reality of a represented action is a step in a process that could undermine or bewilder what one ordinarily thinks of as his sense of reality." This simultaneous avowal and disavowal "boldly asserts the freedom of consciousness itself. The imagination, then, is alternately, or even simultaneously, the supreme instrument of human realization and the eternal snare of delusion of a creature doomed to futility."[9]

In the cinema, too, there is a long tradition of self-reference, ranging from films in which filmmaking itself is part of the subject matter to such films as Keaton's *Sherlock Jr.* (1924) and Vertov's *The Man with a Movie Camera* (1929). In the Keaton film, a movie projectionist dreams himself onto the screen and becomes a character in the very film he is projecting; at the end, back in the projection booth and framed by its opening, he does not know how to behave toward his girlfriend without taking his cues from the images on the screen, which alternate with shots of him as seen through the window of the projection booth. In Vertov's film, we see the very film we are watching being made in front of us; toward the end, the camera itself walks on tripods and takes its bows. Robbe-Grillet's films, like *L'Immortelle* (1963) and *Trans-Europ Express* (1966), are similarly metacinematic. In Godard's *Contempt* (1963) director Fritz Lang provides a metafilmic dimension during the making of a film of Homer's *Odyssey,* and in Godard's *Weekend* (1969) the husband and wife grumble about not liking the film they are in because all they meet are freaks. Such self-reflexiveness is different from the orthodox reflexivity found in the typical Hollywood movie of a movie being made. Contemporary reflexivity in films like *Contempt* and Fellini's *8½* (1963), is not brought to bear on a film within the film, but rather on the film—on film—itself. "In their work, reflexive techniques cause the films to lose their transparency and become themselves the object of the spectator's attention."[10] This kind of reflexivity means that film "is able to reflect not only upon itself as signifying discourse, but also upon its own broader contexts,"[11] the nature of the cinema itself.

Ultimately, the phenomenon of metafictionality, taken in its largest sense to apply not only to works of prose fiction but to any self-reference or self-reflexiveness whether the work be verbal, visual, or aural, forces us to contemplate the nature of the medium in which the work presents itself. We are no longer absorbed by illusion as we were by the realistic novel or the traditional Hollywood narrative film; rather, we are made aware of the power of representation to absorb us, while at the same time we reflect upon the nature of illusion making itself and upon our own perceptual and cognitive abilities to avow or disavow an illusion. All of the works we have glanced at, beginning with the paradigmatic *Don Quixote,* have in common this metafictionality: a self-reflexiveness in which the work of art is made and unmade before our eyes, a constant process of illusion-creating and illusion-destroying, in pursuit of the elusion of illusion.

I have just used two words to which I would like to add a third: *elusion, illusion,* and *allusion. Elusion* means an avoidance of or escape from (detection) by quickness or cunning, *illusion* is something that deceives by producing a false impression, and *allusion* is a casual reference, the incidental mention of something, either by implication or directly; yet they all have a common etymology, from the Latin *ludere,* which means "to play." In providing a context within which to work with Borges' text, I mean to suggest that "Theme of the Traitor and the Hero," like *Don Quixote, Tristram Shandy, The Counterfeiters, Lost in the Funhouse,* and the other examples, plays with its own existence as a literary artifact. It is an allusive story about the elusion of illusion. The story itself demands that we pay attention to its textuality (elusion), its intratextuality (illusion), and its intertextuality (allusion). These terms will serve for analytical purposes, but, as we will see, no simple comparison will work ultimately, especially because these levels intermingle at every point in the text.

In Borges' four-page story there are no fewer than sixteen direct allusions to other texts: mythical, biblical, historical, philosophical, and literary. The story exists in the web of other larger fictions, ranging from the specifically historical (the assassination of Lincoln) to the fictionalization of history (Shakespeare's *Julius Caesar*) to the creation myth itself, the supreme fiction (Hesiod's *Works and Days*). "It is hard," says Robert Scholes, "to see how fiction could insist more resolutely on its fictional character."[12] Ronald Christ sees the device of allusion as a key to the work of Borges: "Allusion unites text and reference in a point of time and space which eliminates both the separateness of the passages and of their authors." To make allusions is "to demonstrate the timeless universality of the human mind."[13] For Borges allusion destroys both linear time and discrete personality; the assassination of Julius Caesar, Abraham Lincoln, and Fergus Kilpatrick are enactments of the same timeless gesture. The story is about illusion. Ryan discovers that historical truth is really false, and that the real truth is false history. Created by Nolan, with the collaboration of Kilpatrick himself and "hundreds of actors," actuality becomes a vast fiction, which in turn becomes actuality recorded: history. As Jaime Alazraki comments, "When the fictitious is converted into historic reality, the historic ... becomes fiction.... Perhaps as an echo of the Shakespearean 'All the world's a stage' or Calderon's *El gran teatro del mundo,* reality is seen as a gigantic performance."[14]

This fiction is perpetuated as history, patterned after literature, yet prefiguring, in the time scheme of the story, a future real event: the death of Lincoln. "Kilpatrick was killed in a theater," Borges writes, "but the entire city was a theater as well, and the actors were legion, and the drama crowned by his death extended over many days and many nights." But ironically, "the passages imitated from Shakespeare are the *least* dramatic." Ryan discovers that history is framed by fiction (STORY→history→STORY) and that fictions are framed by history (HISTORY→story→HISTORY). John O. Stark provides an appropriate image when he suggests "a symmetrical arrangement of two mirrors endlessly reflecting each other with Borges and Shakespeare on the ends, their works inside them, and Ryan in the middle."[15] In the story "Tlön, Uqbar, Orbis Tertius" Borges himself uses such a mirror image when he quotes the encyclopedia text which reads that "the visible universe was an illusion .... Mirrors and fatherhood are abominable because they multiply and disseminate that universe."[16]

Not only was Ryan's decision to publish a book dedicated to the hero's glory foreseen, but Borges' writing of this story, "Theme of the Traitor and the Hero," is part of the spiral of fictions. The tentative fiction Borges wrote is capable of engendering an infinite number of finite fictions, like the one book of "Tlön, Uqbar, Orbis Tertius": "Works of fiction contain a single plot, with all its imaginative permutations. Those of a philosophical nature invariably include both the thesis and the antithesis, the rigorous pro and con of a doctrine. A book which does not contain its counterbook is considered incomplete."[17] For Borges in this story of Fergus Kilpatrick's history, fiction and history are mutually interchangeable counterperceptions; one mirrors and implicates the other. Ryan's decision to "keep his discovery silent" is in fact his contribution to both story and history. To expose the truth, had he decided to do so, would only enlarge the fiction (as Borges is doing by telling us the story of Ryan); it would be as "foreseen" as the book he does write, "dedicated to the hero's glory."

If the story in its intertextuality is allusive and in its intratextuality (its proposed diegesis and the discourse about it, what it plays with) creates illusion, we might say in its textuality it is elusion: not only is the story thematically concerned with the elusiveness of reality, that very theme and the effort of a text to express it are elusive. Reality and actuality, Borges says, constantly elude us, to be replaced by versions of reality whether we call them history, philosophy, biography, or fiction. Fergus Kilpatrick was a betrayer and was executed as a traitor; but he was also a rebel, martyred as a hero. Nolan's orchestration of the hero's death is no less real than Kilpatrick's orchestration of his own betrayal. When we name or label things in actuality, we are counterfeiting reality; no verbalization is ever adequate to the totality of the real or, rather, our perception of the real. Even the very word "real" and the concept behind it are in this sense fictions. To name is to factionalize and to fractionalize: Fergus Kilpatrick is half traitor, half hero. Each is simultaneously true and false. Story is in pursuit of history which in turn pursues and perpetuates story. The only stories we can write are stories about the fictions we cannot avoid being in. We must realize that we are all to some degree collaborators. That is why Borges' text will never, as the narrator of it promises to do "some-day," become more than it is: it is already its story. It plays with us while we play with our fictions of it. All we can do, as Borges is doing with his story, Nolan and Ryan are doing in the story, and I am doing in commenting on the story, is spin fictions. "Metafiction" has emerged rather recently as a term for something that has been an aspect of fiction for a long time, but it is in need of more precise definition as a descriptive term for theory and criticism. For my purposes, I define as metafiction any narrative work (verbal or cinematic) which both in its discourse and story (insofar as these can be separated in analysis) insists on intertextuality for its existence, which in its intratextuality constantly mirrors discourse with story and vice versa, and which in its textuality is finally elusive as a fixed story or discourse. Metafiction rediscovers fiction in its essence; it glories in the powers of narrative. It is not a breakdown of narrative but rather of certain conventional and prescriptive forms of narrative. Despite the high abstract, even valorizing, connotations of the term, metafiction actually restores us to narrative and narrative to us.

Intratextually, Borges' piece is both a story and not a story; it is the story of Kilpatrick but it is simultaneously not that story ("which I shall perhaps write some-day"). It is encoded with traditional narrative elements, plot, character, theme, but fails to meet the reader's expectations of those elements. It is a story about a story, which both does and does not get told, just as *Contempt* and *8½* seem to be films about films that cannot get made and yet are being made in and by the very films we are seeing. Textually, Borges' "Theme of the Traitor and the Hero" defies traditional analytical approaches. Because the story consumes itself in the act of telling, it is elusive—a verbal *ouroboros,* a vicious circle, like a picture of a snake consuming its tail. With its paradoxes and vicious circles, metafiction is both centrifugal and centripetal: it absorbs us in story, but it also distances us so that we see fiction making as an infinite circle. At its most elemental, metafiction as it works in Borges' "Theme of the Traitor and the Hero" enacts and reenacts a primordial scene: we are sitting around the fire and Borges is telling us a story.

When a filmmaker adapts a verbal narrative text, as is so often the case, what is it he is adapting? In the specific case of Borges' "Theme of the Traitor and the Hero," adapted as *The Spider's Stratagem* (*Strategia del ragno*) by Bernardo Bertolucci in 1969, how are verbal and filmic texts related? Though the narrational situation of each is obviously quite different from the other, do we ultimately have the same narrative experience with both, whether we read the story first or watch the film first? Of course, any specific narrative experience, even of the same text on a subsequent reading, is likely to be slightly different from any other; but insofar as we can measure likeness, is the experience of the verbal text more or less identical to the experience of the cinematic text? Does the whole metafictionality of Borges' story emerge from Bertolucci's film as well? Too often in analyzing the relationships between film and literature we limit ourselves by trying to be too literal in measuring the verbal text against its cinematic adaptation; we look for episodes, characters, and subplots that have been left out, put in, or rearranged, and we forget André Bazin's observation that this is only a minor aspect of the problem and that "it is more fruitful to speculate on their differences rather than on their resemblances, that is, for the existence of the novel to be affirmed by the film and not dissolved into it." The emphasis ought to be on the "dialectic between fidelity and creation" which in a film like Bresson's *The Diary of a Country Priest* (1950), an extremely faithful adaptation, can become a dialectic between the cinema and literature. "It is a question of building a secondary work with the novel as foundation. In no sense is the film 'comparable' to the novel or 'worthy' of it. It is a new aesthetic creation, the novel so to speak multiplied by the cinema."[19]

In setting a verbal text next to its cinematic adaptation, we can profitably focus on the differences resulting from what is specific to each medium and, following Bazin, explore the dialectic of film and literature by focusing on the tensions between sameness and difference, between fidelity and creation. We can explore this dialectic in two texts from different media through a modified structural approach since structuralism, as Claude Lévi-Strauss succinctly defines it, "is the quest for the invariant, or for the invariant elements among superficial differences."[20] There has, however, been such a proliferation of terminology from the structural theories and analyses devoted to film and literature that it is impossible to use terms such as "narrative," "story," "discourse," and "narrativity" without creating ambiguity, confusion, overlapping, and even contradiction. Let me, therefore, adapt some terms and define them for my purposes here.[21] In the pure sense, story is an abstraction; it exists independently of any manifestation. That is what makes adaptations from one medium to another possible. A narrative is a medium-specific structure that actualizes a story. A given narrative represents and presents a story, thus absolutely necessitating a narrator whose voice we can identify to a lesser or greater degree even in the most objective of narratives. The relationship between the narrator and the story-as-presented yields the level of discourse, the everything-else that is being communicated in addition to the story-as-represented. Discourse implies readers and viewers who are being communicated with. Narrativity is the process by which a reader (viewer) actively constructs and tries to make meaningful the narrative and discursive levels. Of course, in the reading and viewing process, these levels co-exist; but in analysis, we must separate them in trying to account for the way the specific narrative embodying the story works. We move from story to medium-specificity of narrative, to narration, to discourse, this last level being as unique as the specific text itself; it is the text as experienced. It is the level, as Roland Barthes says, at which the other levels find integration: "the ultimate form of the narrative, as narrative, transcends its contents and its strictly narrative forms (functions and actions)." It is also the level which is not transposable: "What is untranslatable is determined only at the last, narrational level. The signifiers of narrativity, for instance, are not readily transferable from novel to film ...."[22] What is most transposable from Borges' narrative, then, is the story. What is least transferable is its discursive level, along with the narrativity demanded of the reader by the metafictional coding: intrusion of the narrator; allusion (intertextuality); the story being invented as it is being told and yet not told; and other self-reflexive devices such as the spiral of fictions.

What, then, does Bertolucci adapt? Bertolucci's text is indeed faithful to the Borges text on the level of story. This non-manifest story is easy to adapt in verbal or cinematic narrative, and it goes as follows (with full acknowledgement that these five sentences no longer constitute the pure, independent story, but already a minimal narrative): 1) A man has been martyred. 2) History (either oral or written) proclaims and perpetuates him as a hero. 3) Many years later, a descendant investigates the life of that man. 4) He discovers that his ancestor has really been a traitor. 5) He decides to keep his discovery to himself and to preserve the public version of the (hi)story. This five-unit non-manifest story is what is most transposable from Borges' "Theme of the Traitor and the Hero" to Bertolucci's *The Spider's Stratagem.* Let us examine the film on the level of the story-as-represented, moving then to the level of the story-as-presented, and finally to the discourse and narrativity themselves. We will be engaging, to use Barthes' terminology again, in both a horizontal and a vertical reading: "To understand a narrative is not merely to follow the unfolding of the story, it is also to recognize its construction in 'storeys,' to project the horizontal concatenations of the narrative 'thread' on to an implicitly vertical axis; to read (to listen to) a narrative is not merely to move from one word to the next, it is also to move from one level to the next."[23] Understanding a narrative requires both an intralevel "reading" and an interlevel "reading out," the latter meaning a "decoding from surface to deep narrative structures."[24] Narrative translation is possible from one medium to another because roughly the same set of events and existents can be read out.

Borges' text, as we have seen, does not really represent the story it presents; it is synoptic and almost reads like a scenario, something to be represented (which "I shall perhaps write some-day"). In representing the story, Bertolucci has invented his own details for manifestation, but none of these alters the five-unit abstract story. In Borges' text, "the action takes place in an oppressed and tenacious country," Ireland being chosen only for "Narrative convenience." In Bertolucci's text, Fergus Kilpatrick is Athos Magnani, an anti-Fascist killed on June 15, 1936; a bust of him now dominates a square in the small Italian town of Tara, where the action takes place. Some thirty years after Magnani's death, in the present, his son (also named Athos) is called to Tara by his father's mistress, Draifa, after she has seen his picture in a Milan newspaper. The great-grandson (Ryan) in Borges' text here is a son, a difference necessitated by the narrative medium: people alive during the elder Athos' time must still be around to talk to the son. In Borges' text, appropriately, Ryan does his research through books. The Nolan of Borges' text has been multiplied into the three friends of Athos Senior: Gaibazzi (a sausage maker), Rasori (a schoolteacher), and Costa (a movie theater owner). Whereas, in Borges' text, Nolan initiates the fiction of the assassination, in Bertolucci's it is the elder Magnani himself. Borges, also, does not mention the actual drama performed in the theater when Kilpatrick is killed; in the film it is *Rigoletto,* the performance of which is climactic for both Magnanis (it is being performed in the present when Athos Junior finally discovers the truth). Finally, Borges' text gives us no motive for Kilpatrick's treachery; Bertolucci provides one.

In the film, the story-as-represented is fairly straightforward, using flashbacks from four different characters to allow the younger Athos to build the story of his father and discover what happened; that truth, of course, is falsehood. Bertolucci also embeds his represented story in the political and psychological context of Fascism. In an analysis of the film focused primarily on this aspect of the film, Robert Chappetta argues that Bertolucci is criticizing the romantic hero as showman and illusionist, more absorbed in giving the appearance of being a hero than in taking effective action.[25] Thus, for Chappetta, the romantic hero (Athos Senior) carries the seeds of betrayal within him, since the show is always uppermost. He quotes a telling passage from Mussolini's diary: "Hitler and I are a pair of madmen who have given ourselves up to our illusions; our only hope is to create a myth." Indeed, the first time we see Athos Senior, he is indulging in illusions; bragging to his friends that he can make the dawn come early, he crows like a rooster, arousing the real roosters to announce the dawn in the middle of the night. The Italian equivalent for *machismo* is *gallismo,* derived from the word for "rooster." Thus our first glimpse of the elder Athos is that he is living a cock-and-bull story; cows and bulls bellow on the soundtrack thoughout, particularly counterpointing the scenes when the rebels make grandiose, theatrical plans to kill Mussolini, and also in the scene when Athos confesses and Rasori charges him like a bull and Costa rides him (in the latter, we hear, in sharp contrast to the rooster-crow of Athos' first appearance, the sounds of a chicken squawking). When the Fascists play their anthem *Giovinezza* to insult anti-Fascist Magnani, he in turn insults them by dancing to it. But the irony is, as Chappetta makes clear, that "despite his gesture of defiance he is still dancing the Fascist tune." He is like a son in rebellion against his father who, ironically, is much like the father (Mussolini) he is trying to kill. Athos Junior is related to Athos Senior as Athos Senior is related to Mussolini; the son resists but gets trapped in the story, and the father resists Fascism but ends up a collaborator. The son, paralleling his father's assassination attempt, desecrates his father's tomb, but all he destroys is the outward show. His light throws a weblike pattern on the tomb even as he tries to escape the fictional web; in trying to destroy, he too becomes a collaborator. In the final scene, Athos Junior is literally buried in the father's past when the train does not come and the tracks are overgrown with weeds (it is also a mockery of Mussolini's boast that the Facists made the trains run on time). Perhaps the Fascist past is very much present in Italy, as suggested by the likeness of people in past and present; Fascism, like religion, has to be invented and reinvented so that people can have the illusion of resisting what is, after all, an illusion. We note, too, that the name *Athos* suggests *ethos,* the fundamental character or spirit of a culture, the underlying sentiment that informs the beliefs, customs, or practices of a group or society. Looked at this way, Bertolucci's depiction of both the elder and the younger Athos is an indictment of Italian character: the readiness to construct fictions, only to destroy and then reconstruct them. But *Athos* also alludes to the Greek root for atheist, one who believes in nothing and, therefore, perhaps in everything and anything. Magnani is exactly the right name for a man whose theatrical flamboyance can find expression only in an operatic assassination plot. Draifa, whose name evokes a call to justice and freedom, actually wants to imprison. And the town seems frozen in time, populated by old men displaying their machismo, by sexually ambiguous rabbits and children (the scene in which Athos Junior and a boy argue about the sex of the latter's pet rabbit and the scene in which Athos Junior thinks Draifa's young servant is a boy). This ambiguity is echoed in names: Draifa's first name is from a man's last name, and Athos bears a famous woman's last name. In a town that has only the lived illusions of the past and the projected illusions of the future, Athos Junior is the only one who seems to represent the present: the generation that is missing in Tara is precisely that of the younger Athos.

Bertolucci gives a motivation to Athos that is absent from Borges' portrayal of Kilpatrick. Athos betrays because he realizes his impotence. The escaped lion from a German circus, being pursued by men brandishing whips, is fairly docile when we see it the first time, but when Athos looks at it we get a subjective shot in which it is growling ferociously. That same lion is a toothless, stuffed effigy of itself when it is later borne operatically on a platter, as Athos watches soulfully: he sees a mirror image of himself as he would have been but is not. His lion-self has been deflated (by Draifa) but it nourishes (both symbolically and literally, because it is eaten) a new fiction, one in which he will become a hero by first becoming a traitor. Athos Senior can become a hero only by becoming a coward; there is significance in the mirror in front of him when he is killed during the last act of Verdi's *Rigoletto,* the plot of which involves multiple deceptions that backfire on the deceivers. Athos has now become Mussolini: he is being assassinated in the plot intended for Mussolini and, in a sense, has become the thing he wanted to destroy, just as Athos Junior becomes the father he is trying to destroy. We see this in the scene when he is running through the woods and is alternately dressed in his own clothes and in his father's.

Also exploring the Fascist theme of the film, but with a psychoanalytical emphasis, Robert Zaller comments that for Bertolucci "Fascism is as much an historic defect in the Italian national character, a product of Latin bombast, as of textbook Marxist factors."[26] We see that, though the town reveres the image of an anti-Fascist who wasn't really one, it is still under the power of Baccacchia, the overt Fascist who seems to be menacing the younger Athos (the slammed shed door, the punch in the face, the crowd of old men harrassing him). It is Baccacchia who is blamed for the actual murder of Athos Senior, just as he is blamed for Athos Junior's symbolic murder of his father through the desecration of the tomb; but the overt Fascist is actually passive, while the supposed anti-Fascists commit the violent acts. *The Spider's Stratagem* is a film about the complicity between ruler and ruled, on which dictatorship ultimately rests, Zaller argues; tyranny depends on avoidance of freedom and "a collective consent to illusion." In adding Fascism to his story-as-represented, Bertolucci has amplified and multiplied Borges' notion of the spiral of fictions: Fascism is the fiction that breeds all the fictions the characters in the film live by.

In addition to these studies of the film's politics, the film invites Lacanian psychoanalytic investigation; it is, as many reviewers pointed out, very much like a dream. Bertolucci has said that he made the film "in a state of melancholic happiness and great serenity,"[27] calling the film "a sort of psychoanalytic therapy, a journey through the realm of pre-conscious memory."[28] We have done a fairly traditional analysis of some of the possible meanings of the story-as-represented in the film. Bertolucci is certainly faithful to the story, but in adding the Fascist context he is also being creative: his depiction of Fascism reinforces the illusion and the elusiveness of (hi)story that are at the heart of Borges' text. It seems that in adaptation it is the traditional elements that get transposed—the story, its plot, characters, setting, and theme. If Bertolucci were merely a literal adapter, he would have no trouble with Borges' text, and he in fact does not; he treats it as a scenario and fleshes it out in a medium-specific narrative. Precisely the metafictional dimensions of the Borges text interest him: the dimensions that involve the narrator, discourse, and narrativity, levels least transposable from one medium to another.

In examining these levels, we, in Barthes' words, "describe the code by which narrator and reader are signified throughout the narrative itself."[29] In narrating his story, Bertolucci creates a film that is as intertextual as Borges' text. Like Borges, Bertolucci uses allusion: historical (Mussolini, Dreyfus), musical (Schoenberg, Verdi's *Rigoletto* and *A Masked Ball*), literary (Shakespeare, Victor Hugo's *Hernani*) and theatrical (Magnani). There are allusions to the visual arts: Bertolucci composes some of his frames to evoke the early work of Giorgio de Chirico, whose sterile colonnaded streets, sliced by sharp shadows and cold sunlight, suggest some ominous mystery (see especially *Nostalgia of the Infinite*, 1913; *The Mystery and Melancholy of a Street*, 1914; and *Metaphysical Landscape*, 1929). Toward the end of the film there is a scene in the square with umbrella-holding men and women that evokes René Magritte's *Golconda* (1953). Bertolucci has said that he showed his cinematographer Vittorio Storaro some Magritte paintings, especially *The Empire of Light*, to explain how he wanted the film to look.[30] Toward the end, the younger Athos alludes to a line from Borges himself: "No one is anyone, one single immortal man is all men."[31] When the townspeople listen to the opera piped outside through loudspeakers, we catch sight of a stooped, silhouetted man leaning on a cane, who may well be an allusion to Borges himself. Bertolucci alludes to other films (*Gone with the Wind*, and those of the movie posters we see in the scene at Costa's outdoor movie theater) as well.

The narrative self-reflexiveness of Borges' fiction finds creative expression in Bertolucci's composition of the frame. Almost every shot is a flourish, emphasizing the camera filming as much as the contents of the frame. "For me," Bertolucci has said, "the cinema is an art of gestures.... I move the camera as if I was gesturing with it."[32] In the outdoor movie theater, when a giant screen is rolled up to reveal lush vegetation behind it, Bertolucci is playing with his medium in the same way that Borges does with his: he is letting us see the screen behind the illusion that is the projected image, and then rolling up the screen to reveal actuality, as though the screen we are watching were also being rolled up. In this scene, Bertolucci is self-reflexive not only toward his own film but toward the cinema as such with its powers of illusion, just as Borges in his verbal narrative reveals the storying and de-storying powers of narrative. As Christian Metz points out: what unfolds on the screen may be more or less fictional, "but the unfolding is itself fictive." Thus "every film is a fiction film."[33] The signifier itself is recorded, is not there.

Throughout the film, characters are framed: by colonnades, in windows, in mirrors, by the boxes at the theater, against pictures and murals, down corridors and streets. In the flashback scene when the elder Magnani creates his fiction, he is silhouetted against and framed within a series of arches, beyond which the town of Tara looks like a technicolor stage set. Sometimes the camera remains stationary while characters walk out of, then back into, the frame. There is much tracking and panning, the latter emphasizing the circularity of the story as well as of the narration, as in the 360° pan when Athos Junior first arrives at Draifa's vine-covered villa, and in the use of subjective camera when Athos looks at his father's statue. The camera does not revolve around the statue; the statue revolves with the camera, its blank eyes always facing Athos at the same angle. In the flashback when Athos Senior is told the news that Mussolini is coming to Tara, he turns slowly toward us, like a statue on a revolving pedestal, and says, "We must kill him." It is the beginning of the circular story he creates for himself.

In another flashback, when Draifa encircles the elder Athos in bandages, another vicious circle is enacted on the level of discourse. On the level of story-as-represented, Draifa's telling Athos Senior he is a coward makes him see the hollowness of his anti-Fascist heroism and psychologically probably motivates his betrayal of the assassination plot. In the present, Draifa's first reception of Athos into her villa involves her circling around him several times; and later, when she tells him "You can't go away anymore," she puts the father's jacket on him as the camera follows them into a semicircular corridor. The mosquito coil she lights is another spiral. The whole town of Tara seems to be encircled by a highway—beyond which we may assume there is a real world. The town of Tara has decided to stop particpating in actuality since it created its own illusion of reality on the day Athos Senior was killed. The town is a stage set which Bertolucci's camera brings to life. Early in the film, when the younger Athos looks at the sign of a street named after his father, the camera reads from right to left along "VIA ATHOS MAGNANI," signalling us that Athos Junior is on a journey back in time that will lead him to his father—will make him simultaneous with his father. But, more significantly, on the discursive level of the film this is also a sign of reading, calling our attention to the reading of the film itself, to the circling from story to discourse to story to discourse.

Having the actors portray themselves in time present and time past without any changes in makeup to denote youth or age further emphasizes the indistinguishability to past from the present, the illusory from the real; but it calls attention as well, again on the discursive level, to Bertolucci's departure from classical narrative films which seek to hide their codes of narrativity. As Barthes points out, "our society takes the greatest pains to conjure away the coding of the narrative situation .... The reluctance to declare its codes characterizes bourgeois society and the mass culture issuing from it: both demand signs which do not look like signs."[34] Bertolucci, like Borges in his text, overtly codes the narrative situation in a way that forces the viewer into a more active narrativity than he is asked to perform in a traditional film.

Other aspects of the film's discourse and narrativity separate it from classical narrative films while emphasizing its self-reflexivity: the punctuation, the use of the displaced diegetic insert, and the final shot. There were twelve fades in the film, six of which occur in rapid succession within a single syntagmatic unit: when Gaibazzi talks to Athos Junior while inspecting the sausages. No really significant time elapses during each one; they call attention to themselves as cinematic punctuation rather than easing us into a different unit of narrative. While almost no time is passing in each brief segment, Bertolucci discursively emphasizes that a great deal of time has passed. Gaibazzi's story is continuous, but the fades disrupt it, fragmenting it until we are aware of a story being told diegetically and of the film's telling of that telling. In the film, there is constant storytelling within the story (the flashbacks of the three friends, Draifa, and Baccacchia). Bertolucci is telling the story of Athos Junior, who in turn—along with us—is being told the story of Athos Senior, who in turn created (lived) a story of his own making, which in turn entraps Athos Junior in its plot. This story of stories (and of storeys) expands until there seems to be no dividing line between reality and fiction, between history and story; yet, as a finite narrative structure, *The Spider's Stratagem* must contain this expansion within its own physical duration. The film calls attention to itself narrating while Gaibazzi is narrating part of the story that the film is narrating. In addition to the twelve fades, there are four dissolves in the film (not counting the credits), three used conventionally to move to flashback, but one shows a simultaneous image of the boy at the hotel setting down a tray and lying on the bed, both within the same frame setup. This dissolve, which has no real diegetic purpose except to indicate a little time passing, is entirely too obtrusive and calls our attention to the film itself, to the film narrating, to the film discoursing, and thus to the viewer's need for active narrativity: the traditionally transparent codes of transition here become opaque signifiers themselves, signifiers of metafiction.

The displaced diegetic insert is defined by Metz as "an image that, while remaining entirely 'real,' is displaced from its normal filmic position."[35] Such an insert occurs first in shot three of the film, then four times in alternation with the flashback of Athos Senior's confession, and next to the last shot of the film; it also occurs twice at night, only once as part of the diegetic action. In all, it occurs eight times as a displaced insert. The shot is across a cornfield and the building appears to be the theater, which, from this angle, dominates Tara, is Tara. Who sees this image? It can't be Athos, given his position when the image is inserted. This is an autonomous shot, emphasizing the narration itself and thus, again, forcing the viewer through narrativity to examine the discursive level of the film. This displaced diegetic insert moves us as spectators from the diegesis to narration and finally to discourse and narrativity; it makes us conscious of the film as film and inscribes disavowal into our very avowal of the film's illusion.

The last shot of the film, a traveling shot of railway tracks, evokes the first when the train arrived and Athos disembarked after the thud of the sailor's bag on the platform (the sailor gets off after Athos). The sailor, a troublesome character because he is never seen again until just before the end of the film and has nothing to do with the story that unfolds and entraps, is functional only on the discursive level—he is the viewer in the text. The thud of his bag is our investment in the story just as it starts. In the second shot of the film the sailor is meandering behind Athos as the latter walks toward camera from the station; suddenly, the sailor stops, executes a sharp military step behind Athos, cutting a definite path between the station and Athos. Then he sits down on a bench (as we sit in our movie seat?), opens his arms, and says "Tara!" as though to say, "Here is your stage; let your story begin." The next shot (shot 3) is the first use of the displaced diegetic insert: the theater dominating Tara. The sailor leaves the film just at the point when Athos Junior is about to be entrapped in the story, which, as he tells Draifa before leaving her, "no longer interests me." Athos has already been lured back from the platform when the sailor rushes past and shouts goodbye. When he leaves, we too, in a sense, leave the story and enter the discourse. At the very end, Athos' bag (which he had earlier forgotten at the station) is left standing as he surveys the grass and weeds overgrowing the tracks. These tracks are the means of coming and going into Tara, into and out of the film that creates Tara. The camera that read the street sign right to left now moves left to right, returning us (but not Athos) to where he and we came from. The story is ended: there is closure to the diegesis, but the filmic discourse opens up here to its widest. The story (screen as space filled in by narrative) is over; the discourse (screen as mirror, self-reflexive, looking at us as we look at it) takes over and simultaneously lets us in on and frees us from the narrative rendering.

We are released from a fictional web in which we have been as completely trapped, in a sense, as Athos Senior and Junior in theirs. Athos Junior swallows the story and is swallowed up in it. He is the film's negative image of the kind of viewer the film demands: one who maintains the balance between distanciation and appropriation. For Athos Junior the story has become simultaneously a discovery and an entrapment; his role is fated in the fiction, and he cannot get out of the fiction of his fate.[36] We the viewers are released from the story, at least from this particular story, in order to contemplate, on the discursive level, the power that fictions have over us. Christian Metz has observed that "behind any fiction there is a second fiction: the diegetic events are fictional, that is the first; but everyone pretends to believe they are true, and that is the second."[37] *The Spider's Stratagem* disturbs us not only for its troubling excursus into the problematics of illusion; it is disturbing precisely because we have watched the film. Its fixing us for 97 minutes in its duration is itself the stratagem.

The ultimate signified of *The Spider's Stratagem* is this film itself in its fictive power.

It is true that Bertolucci's film is not metafictional in the overtly frame-breaking way that *Sherlock Jr.* and *The Man with the Movie Camera* are, just as Borges' text is hardly a piece of flamboyantly experimental fiction, the kind in which we shuffle the pages at random, or plough through seven sets of quotation marks (as in John Barth's "Menelaiad" in *Lost in the Funhouse*). This kind of experimental narrative, or surfiction,[38] is a special kind of metafiction, one which seeks to break new ground in radical ways. The type of metafiction we have been examining in Borges and Bertolucci is more indirect, more in the tradition of Cervantes than of Vertov. Borges and Bertolucci insist on traditional narrative structure: both texts, after all, tell stories with a beginning, middle, and end; there is also plot, theme, and characterization of varying degree. *The Spider's Stratagem*, nevertheless, is more metafictional than films like Wilder's *Sunset Boulevard* (1950), Kelly and Donen's *Singin' in the Rain* (1952), Minnelli's *Two Weeks in Another Town* (1962), Truffaut's *Day for Night* (1973), and Schlesinger's *The Day of the Locust* (1975). These films are reflective of filmmaking, but they are not self-reflexive, except incidentally. Making films is part of the closed diegesis of each. Their narratives are conventionally transparent and employ none of the frame-breaking codes Bertolucci uses to make *The Spider's Stratagem* not only reflective but self-reflexive as well. These films are examples of orthodox reflexivity, while Bertolucci's film is an example of modernist reflexivity. The difference between the two modes is the same as the difference between James's "The Lesson of the Master" (1888) or Mann's *Death in Venice* (1911) and Borges' "Theme of the Traitor and the Hero" or Barth's *Funhouse* stories. The former are reflective, certainly, and reflexive in a conventional way, while the latter are reflective, reflexive, and self-reflexive.

The same relationship that exists between *The Spider's Stratagem* and "Theme of the Traitor and the Hero" exists between Antonioni's *Blow-Up* (1966) and the Cortázar story from which it is adapted ("Blow-Up" in English but "Las babas del diablo" or "The Devil's Drool" in Spanish). The film *Blow-Up* has been described as "a series of photographs about a series of photographs" which constitutes "what might be called a metalinguistic metaphor, a highly self-conscious and self-reflexive meditation on its own process."[39] *Blow-Up* and "Blow-Up" and "Theme of the Traitor and the Hero" and *The Spider's Stratagem* are metafictional in the same way; without violently breaking from traditional narrative, they nevertheless manage to make narration and fiction making their central concern. That is how they are self-reflexive. They portray a world and themselves; they are consciously stories and self-consciously not stories: "The world of the self-conscious artwork is the world in which artist and audience confront each other across a proscenium both know to be 'true' but deliberately agree to consider 'false'; however, as neither is allowed to forget the fiction of fiction, both continually probe the truth of their encounter, as well as the truth of the lie that accepts its falsehood. The dynamics of this confrontation give rise to the illusion that the work is aware of itself, directs itself, conceives itself: that a self-conscious film, for instance, can be its own mindscreen."[40]

In putting Borges' text on film, Bertolucci, like Borges in his text, has made a fiction on fiction. The process is not a matter of simply looking for cinematic equivalents for verbal narrative and discursive elements; it is a matter of exploring the range from fidelity to creation, of seeing how faithfulness to story can be accompanied by a creative and inventive dimension that multiplies, to use Bazin's term, story and discourse. Just as Borges' text is a performance of self-assured virtuosity, so Bertolucci uses a self-conscious camera style that emphasizes the very showiness his film is thematically criticizing. He glories in the power of film to create illusion and to make us avow; yet, on the discursive level, he signals us also to disavow: there is danger in the pleasure of illusion. Borges' text partakes of a metafictionality that is as old as the novel itself, and Bertolucci's text uses metafictional devices that have existed since the beginnings of cinema. In talking about modernist cinema, Metz makes just this point when he says: "The new cinema, far from having abandoned the narrative, gives us narratives that are more diversified, more ramified, and more complex."[41] Borges in "Theme of the Traitor and the Hero," Bertolucci in *The Spider's Stratagem,* restore narrative to us through a metafictional presentation and through the narrativity this demands of us.

*University of Maine at Orono*

## NOTES

[1] "Tema del traidor y del héroe" (1944), trans. James E. Irby, in Jorge Luis Borges, *Labyrinths: Selected Stories and Other Writings* (New York: New Directions, 1964), pp. 72-75.

[2] Margaret Heckard, "Robert Coover, Metafiction, and Freedom," *Twentieth Century Literature,* 22 (1976), 215.

[3] André Gide, *The Counterfeiters,* trans. Dorothy Bussy (New York: Random House, 1927), p. 205.

[4] John Barth, *Lost in the Funhouse* (New York: Doubleday, 1968), p. 114.

[5] Borges, *Labyrinths,* p. 25.

[6] William Gass, *Fiction and the Figures of Life* (New York: Knopf, 1970), pp. 24-25, 109.

[7] Roland Barthes, *S/Z,* trans. Richard Miller (New York: Hill and Wang, 1974), pp. 4-5.

[8] Robert Scholes, "Metafiction," *Iowa Review,* 1 (1970), 106. This is now incorporated into his *Fabulation and Metafiction* (Urbana: Univ. of Illinois Press, 1979), pp. 105-23. For Scholes, *fabulation* is the larger term and *metafiction* but one of its forms: "Fabulation . . . means not a turning away from reality, but an attempt to find more subtle correspondences between the reality which is fiction and the fiction which is reality" (p. 8).

[9] Robert Alter, *Partial Magic: The Novel as a Self-Conscious Genre* (Berkeley: Univ. of California Press, 1975), pp. 15, 18.

[10] William C. Siska, "Metacinema: A Modern Necessity," *Literature/Film Quarterly,* 7 (1979), 285-89.

[11] Don Fredericksen, "Modes of Reflexive Film," *Quarterly Review of Film Studies,* 4 (1979), 307.

[12] Robert Scholes, *Elements of Fiction* (New York: Oxford Univ. Press, 1968), p. 84.

[13] Ronald Christ, *The Narrow Act: Borges' Art of Illusion* (New York: New York Univ. Press, 1969), pp. 34, 35.

[14] Jaime Alazraki, *Jorge Luis Borges* (New York: Columbia Univ. Press, 1971), pp. 36-37. See also Howard D. Pearce, "A Phenomenological Approach to the *Theatrum Mundi* Metaphor," *PMLA*, 95 (1980), 42-57: "The audience and playwright and play and characters are accomplices in making and sharing a world of meaning according to the rules of their game" (p. 56).

[15] John O. Stark, *The Literature of Exhaustion: Borges, Nabokov, and Barth* (Durham, N.C.: Duke Univ. Press, 1974), p. 15.

[16] Borges, *Labyrinths*, p. 4 (italics in the original).

[17] Borges, *Labyrinths*, p. 13.

[18] For a selective bibliographical survey see my "Literature/Film: A Bibliography," *Literature/Film Quarterly*, 6 (1978), 135-43 and especially James Goodwin, "Literature and Film: A Review of Criticism," *Quarterly Review of Film Studies*, 4 (1979), 227-46.

[19] André Bazin, "The Stylistics of Robert Bresson," *What Is Cinema?* ed. and trans. Hugh Gray (Berkeley: Univ. of California Press, 1967), pp. 143, 142.

[20] Claude Lévi-Strauss, *Myth and Meaning* (New York: Schocken, 1979), p. 8.

[21] I am adapting my terms mostly from Seymour Chatman, *Story and Discourse: Narrative Structure in Fiction and Film* (Ithaca, N.Y.: Cornell Univ. Press, 1978), pp. 37, 20, 41, and Robert Scholes, "Narration and Narrativity in Film," *Quarterly Review of Film Studies*, 1 (1976), 283, 285, 286. See also Dudley Andrew, "The Structuralist Study of Narrative: Its History, Use, and Limits," *The Bulletin of the Midwest Modern Language Association*, 8 (1975), 45-61.

[22] Roland Barthes, "Introduction to the Structural Analysis of Narratives," *Image, Music, Text*, trans. Stephen Heath (New York: Hill and Wang, 1977), pp. 115, 121.

[23] Barthes, "Introduction," p. 87.

[24] Chatman, p. 41.

[25] Robert Chappetta, "The Meaning Is Not the Message," *Film Quarterly*, 25 (Summer 1972), 10-18.

[26] Robert Zaller, "Bernardo Bertolucci, Or Nostalgia for the Present," *The Massachusetts Review*, 16 (1975), 807-28.

[27] Amos Vogel, "Bernardo Bertolucci: An Interview," *Film Comment*, 7 (Fall, 1971), 26.

[28] Richard Roud, "Fathers and Sons," *Sight and Sound*, 40 (Spring 1971), 61.

[29] Barthes, "Introduction," p. 110.

[30] "Dialogue on Film: Bernardo Bertolucci,"*American Film*, 5 (January-February 1980), 41.

[31] Borges, "The Immortal," *Labyrinths*, pp. 114-15.

[32] Vogel, p. 26.

[33] Christian Metz, "The Imaginary Signifier," *Screen*, 16, 2 (Summer 1975), 47.

[34] Barthes, "Introduction," p. 116.

[35] Christian Metz, *Film Language: A Semiotics of the Cinema*, trans. Michael Taylor (New York: Oxford Univ. Press, 1974), p. 125.

[36] See Donald G. Marshall, "Plot as Trap; Plot as Mediation," *The Bulletin of the Midwest Modern Language Association*, 10 (1977), 11-28.

[37] Metz, "The Imaginary Signifier," p. 70.

[38] See Raymond Federman, ed., *Surfiction: Fiction Now and Tomorrow* (Chicago: Swallow Press, 1975).

[39] John Freccero, "Blow-Up: From the Word to the Image," *Yale/Theatre*, 3 (Fall 1970), 15-24. Also see Terry J. Peavler, "*Blow-Up:* A Reconsideration of Antonioni's Infidelity to Cortázar," *PMLA*, 94 (1979), 887-93.

[40] Bruce F. Kawin, *Mindscreen: Bergman, Godard, and First-Person Film* (Princeton, N.J.: Princeton Univ. Press, 1978), pp. 50-51.

[41] Metz, *Film Language,* p. 227.

# Strick's Adaptation of Joyce's
## *Portrait of the Artist:*
# Discourse and Containing Discourse

### MICHAEL KLEIN

In writing *Temptation,* Flaubert produced the first literary work whose exclusive domain is that of books... and modern literature is activated: Joyce ... Kafka, Pound, Borges. The library is on fire.[1]

Michel Foucault

Foucault offers a provocative assessment of the shift away from mimesis in modern writing.[2] Yet the self-reflection which he notes is, while characteristic, only part of the story. History lies behind the literary facade of modernism in James Joyce, Franz Kafka, Ezra Pound, and Jorge Luis Borges. In the final sense, the works reflect not only their own processes but the processes of their times. This is especially clear in Joyce's *Dubliners,* but perhaps is less obvious in *A Portrait of the Artist as a Young Man,* where the subjective point of view and Stephen Dedalus' neo-Platonic aesthetic color or filter out (and this in the turbulent years immediately preceding the Easter uprising) the intense contradictions of Irish society. However, whereas in the novel Joyce's prose presents the external world filtered through Stephen's consciousness, in the film of the novel Joseph Strick's camera records both Stephen's consciousness and the panorama of the external world with its social and historical implications. Thus we receive a double vision, or two discourses: one critical of Ireland and its culture, the other nationalist and affirmative. In doing this Strick allies his own point of view with the mimetic, inclusive nature of the camera's eye, which disinterestedly records both background and foreground simultaneously, situating the subjective in its place within the larger event or narrative. In this way the containing discourse of Strick's film expands our perspective on the novel. Thus although the film takes the novel as its "domain," to use Foucault's term, in doing so it moves away from, rather than towards, modernism's self-conscious concern with artifice, to situate the original work in actuality, in history.

Dorothy Van Ghent has called our attention to some of the reasons for Joyce's shift away from mimesis in the final revised draft of his autobiographical novel: "In a stable culture, the artist inherits certain broad assumptions as to the nature of reality which, in some degree, correspond with empirical experience of the kind of relationships people maintain with themselves, and with each other, and with their natural environment.... But in a time of cultural crisis, when ... all reality is ... thrown into question, the mind turns inward on itself to seek the shape of reality there ...."[3] In *Portrait,* as Stephen begins to rebel, first against his family and his Irish

Catholic upbringing and then against the provincial aspects of Irish nationalism, the world of Ireland tends to fade more and more into the background. As Stephen becomes increasingly self-involved, Joyce's novel abandons traditional narrative structure (a character placed in a net of social relations) and internalizes external action. Stephen's world becomes subjective—his own creation, a discourse. This process may be traced through Joyce's text. When Stephen was a child, the primary historical events of the time (the betrayal of Parnell, the re-emergence of the Irish nationalist cause) were directly assimilated into his consciousness: he eavesdropped, looked at and listened to the adult world. However, as Stephen's consciousness actively develops in his school years and later, Ireland becomes an idea in his mind, a negative conception which he rejects (*"non-serviam"*). Apart from the famous scenes of epiphany, whose significance lies not so much in their beauty as in their arousal of Stephen's sense of artistic vocation, the natural and the social landscapes of Ireland tend to fade from the book. The novel gives us a jagged mosaic, fragments of Stephen's mind. At the conclusion of Joyce's text Stephen leaves Ireland proclaiming "Welcome O life!" However, reality has become the Ideal: "I desire to press in my arms the loveliness which has not yet come into the world."[4]

Several years ago Mary McCarthy suggested that we have been misreading *Portrait*.[5] We have made the mistake of regarding Stephen as a reliable narrator and hence have wrongly granted his discourse significant authority. One might extend this suggestion and read the novel as a work of irony in which Stephen's cultural, aesthetic, and political performances are to be regarded as merely solipsistic. Strick's film of Joyce's text doesn't go this far: he includes a good deal of Joyce's language and much of Stephen's perspective. However, he repeatedly shifts the point of view, making a realistic and objective work out of Joyce's montage of subjective fragments; the Irish landscape, the Irish social scene, Irish folk music, and minor or background characters (Simon Dedalus, Stephen's mother, Davin, Cranly) become rival signs, as authentic and authoritative as Stephen's discourse. The result is a double vision: on the one hand, Stephen's modernist cosmopolitan rebellion; on the other, the cultural and political claims of Ireland.

The narrative of Strick's film proceeds chronologically, relating Joyce's story of Stephen Dedalus from childhood to young manhood: Stephen's babyhood memories; his witness of family debates about the Irish cause and the Church's betrayal of Parnell; his early schooling; his intense religious conversion and subsequent decision not to become a priest; his sexual initiation; his rejection of the traditional Irish radical movement; his dedication to Art and exile from Ireland, home and family. Joyce's perspective is faithfully rendered through Stephen's actions, statements to his friends, and journal entries, and by means of the narrator (the voice-over which is Stephen's voice); thus Stephen continues, in the film as in the novel, to be Joyce's vehicle. Throughout the film most of the dialogue is transposed from Joyce's text, so that Stephen's voice and his pronouncements about art and life in Ireland and the provincial and repressive aspects of Irish culture are retained with few cuts.

However, there is an additional level of discourse in the film, so that, despite Stephen, the Ireland which he rejects asserts its presence. This is brought about by various means. At times it is simply a matter of duration. For example, the Christmas dinner scene, in which Stephen's father and his companions castigate England and the Church and defend Parnell and the Irish cause while young Stephen listens wide-eyed, takes up considerably more time in the film than it does in the novel, and thus it gains greater emphasis. The scene is both humorous and pointed. When Simon Dedalus praises the martyred Parnell, eats the "Pope's nose" with a flourish, glances at his son, and calls for Irish independence from both England and the Church, we watch Stephen and we observe with Stephen. But here, in the film, we are not solely dependent on Stephen's vision; because the camera pictures or renders the presence of Stephen's father and his companions to a greater extent than their dialogue does in Joyce's text, they come alive and they and their views gain independent authority. In general, all the background characters who speak for Ireland and Irish culture have a greater presence in the film, in part because we see them so that they are dramatically present for a sustained period independent of Stephen's voice.

The Irish discourse also asserts itself in the film in ways independent of the narrative. The music (often orchestrated renditions of Irish folk tunes) works rhetorically to evoke a positive sense of Irish traditional culture. At times it does this in contradiction to the narrative or to Stephen's narrative voice. Similarly, the insistent background of the landscape situates the action: Strick's film abounds with glorious visions of the Irish countryside, of congenial vistas of the old houses and streets, of the doors and lanes of Dublin. In a sense, the film is a period piece, a historical recreation, self-consciously encoded by the director to arouse traditional responses. The iconic presence of Ireland, the physical beauty that Joyce assimilates and criticizes in Stephen's discourse, is instead manifested directly in Strick's film as a sign of value.[6] This occurs in part because it is natural for the camera eye to include surrounding physical reality as the background of scenes that are set out of doors or within specific historical locations. The dress, architecture, and style of turn-of-the-century Ireland, recreated, photographed in depth, and set in motion in film, transmit values that modify and contain the perceptions of the novel's central protagonist. Further, the mise-en-scène of the film directs our attention to the background by numerous establishing shots, by maintaining depth of focus or by supplementing Stephen's voice on the sound track. While Stephen is in the foreground of the frame we are very aware of Ireland around him, even as, while listening to his voice, we hear the folk ballads, the plaintive strains of the tradition he is single-mindedly rejecting.

Strick follows this structure most noticeably in the final scenes. Joyce's text has Stephen setting down his thoughts in his journal shortly before leaving Ireland: "24 March. Began with a discussion with my mother. Subject: B. V. M. . . . Mother indulgent. Said I have a queer mind and have read too much. . . . Cannot repent. Told her so and asked for sixpence. Got threepence" (p. 248). In the novel the scene is completely interiorized. Thus Joyce does not set it in a specific location; Harry Levin has noted that as *Portrait* "advances, it becomes less sensitive to outside impressions, and more intent upon speculations of its own."[7] The scene is also presented exclusively from Stephen's point of view, and at the end of the journal entry, Stephen concludes that the Irish are "a race of clodhoppers!" (p. 249).

However, in Strick's film the scene is externalized and objectified. On the one hand, Stephen is heard stating a fair amount of the journal entry. But there is also a counter discourse. We hear the sound of a harp playing Irish music. We see Stephen's mother at work in the sunlit garden in back of their house, listening to Stephen, but also preoccupied with hoeing the ground. We see several of Stephen's brothers and sisters, sympathetic close-ups of their young faces near a shed, in the garden in back of their house. We see in close-up a plant sprouting out of the freshly turned soil. As Stephen continues speaking (the voice-over) his words are further situated by a montage of typical iconic scenes: the Irish coast, the green fields in spring, old men drinking in a pub. While Joyce's text presents only Stephen's vision, Strick's film gives us Stephen's words and situates these words within an environment that is both the source of his rebellion and the source of a counter or containing discourse. The result is an objectified configuration of signs: Stephen's discourse; the country and culture that he rejects; and the physical, cultural, and social claims of that world.

To take another example: "5 April. Wild spring. Scudding clouds. O life! Dark stream of swirling bogwater on which appletrees have cast down their delicate flowers" (p. 250). In Joyce's text, Stephen rhapsodizes about spring, but quickly hypostatizes nature into a symbolic image of life, into an epiphany. In Strick's film, the scene is set in Stephen's small room. While he speaks of life he is visually objectified or placed by the camera's eye in his dark study—enclosed, isolated, and alienated. We sense the future, the personal cost of exile. Joyce's text concludes with Stephen's voice: "Welcome, O life! I go to encounter for the millionth time the reality of experience and to forge in the smithy of my soul the uncreated conscience of my race" (pp. 252-53). In Strick's film, again, the scene is objectified, that is, set in definite physical, social, and historical relations. We see Stephen getting on a boat together with an assorted group of tourists and travelers, all en route to France via England. The camera pans up from a portrait of an eighteenth-century English regal figure on the boat to Stephen standing on the deck, suggesting that his journey away from Ireland to transcendence begins, concretely, perhaps questionably, on an English boat.

Nonetheless, in these scenes Strick is not satirizing Stephen or negating his vision but rather qualifying it. We perceive two discourses: there is no resolution. The Irish discourse only supplements Joyce's text, and thus renders Stephen's quandary, clearly establishing the basis of historical and cultural contradictions that lie behind Joyce's early work. By exploring the resources of film (in particular, the multifaceted quality of deep focus documentary-style images) Strick situates Joyce's third person limited narrative in a larger or containing context. The result, in its objectivity and inclusiveness, is more like Balzac than early Joyce, more realist than modernist. Although much of the intensity and virtuosity of Joyce's youthful modernism is lessened (Strick's film doesn't blaze like Joyce's book), the work is nonetheless significant as a recreation of the situation that brought

Joyce's text forth—as a portrait, deceptively traditional in style, of *A Portrait of the Artist*.

Robert Scholes, in discussing "narration and narrativity in film" has commented that cinema combines the essential qualities of both narrative literature ("verbal narrative") and visual art ("pictorial representation"), qualities that G. E. Lessing contrasted in his *Laokoon*.[8] This definition can be further expanded. Film, being an encyclopedic and synthesizing art form, combines aspects of literature (fiction, drama, poetry), music, mime, dance, architecture, and photography as well as painting.[9] Indeed the composite nature of film has been assumed in my discussion of *Portrait of the Artist* as novel and as film, especially in the account of the function of encoded music and landscape in the film.

Pictorial representation may be both mimetic and expressive and thus a source of meaning. This is often true of other aspects of film as well. André Bazin has called attention to the ways in which the camera reproduces, situates, and frames narrative action;[10] Béla Balázs to the iconic function of images of the human face;[11] George Bluestone to the complexity of visual tropes in motion pictures;[12] and Sergei Eisenstein to the analytic and emotional possibilities of montage of spatial, tonal, and cognitive elements.[13] Camera position and angle, camera movement, framing, lighting, and visual and aural editing are, perhaps, the primary means by which a director may reproduce, shape, and thus express and evaluate the significance of a series of events or a narrative. In addition, film often gives primacy to a range of supra-mimetic historical signs (costume, architecture, customs—the documentary record of a culture, class, nation, or period in all its qualities), objects with significance, hieroglyphs that are more than a source of verisimilitude for they are pregnant with value and meaning. These are an inherent part of the secondary field or background of an image whether a film is made on location or on a set, unless a director intervenes to blur or screen out their presence by using special lighting or focal lengths to abstract the action from its containing cultural, social, and physical environment.

Background may, of course, be understood both literally and figuratively. When we comment on the role of music in a film, we often refer to it as the musical background. In a sense the total visual and aural configuration, apart from the action and dialogue of the narrative, can be thought of as background. Bazin touches on this question in his discussion of deep focus in his essay "The Evolution of the Language of the Cinema."[14] Deep focus, or depth of field, like foreground/background, is more than a literal description of space in a frame of film. Deep focus in modern film is more than just a visual effect achieved as a result of technological innovations which enabled both the foreground and the background of an image to be brought together into clear focus. The fact of depth involves simultaneity, the simultaneous perception of a multitude of objects, signs and relations in the image on the screen by the spectator.[15] By convention most often the main narrative events are situated in the foreground and a configuration of secondary elements in the background, the latter noted in passing or virtually sensed subliminally. Both foreground and background may constitute distinct discourses. At times the emphasis may shift dialectically; elements of the configuration in the background may overdetermine and contain the material in the foreground. The complex interaction of foreground and background, of discourse and containing discourse, mirrors the complex relations of experience which are the common subject of significant literature and film. In the film of *Portrait of the Artist,* as I have indicated, the music, landscape, and a related cluster of signs (the Irish discourse) contain, that is, in this case, modify and qualify, the discourse of Stephen, the major character in the narrative.

The primacy of containing discourse, far from being uncommon, is indeed a defining trait of a range of films, and to a lesser extent, of certain modern forms of literature. When the film is based upon a literary narrative, the comparison may be especially interesting. Containing discourse functions with varying degrees of presence, in different ways in different films, and in differing ways within a given film: it may modify or qualify a significant narrative; may in itself be the primary source of meaning in a film; or may simply amplify a significant narrative, heightening certain moments. The film of *Portrait of the Artist* is an illustration of the first sort. Joyce's novel, although ironic in some respects, is primarily a *Bildungsroman.* The author has minimized his presence as a guide to the reader, and Stephen's thoughts, statements, and actions are the primary signposts of value. However, in Strick's film, as we have seen, Joyce's narrative and Stephen's monologues and soliloquies are contained within a discourse that modifies and qualifies Stephen's critique of Ireland and affirms the best values of the Irish nation and culture.

In Stanley Kubrick's film *Barry Lyndon,* to cite an example of the second sort, the containing discourse is in itself the primary location of meaning. Thackeray's novel, the source of the film, is an ironic account of the life of Barry Lyndon. Through a number of narrative devices (ironic inflation of Barry's self-reflective first-person narration, inclusion of other characters' negative estimates of Barry, footnotes appended to the narrative by the author), Barry's actions in the novel are placed in critical perspective. However, in Kubrick's minimalist film, value-indicating aspects of the narrative are reduced virtually to zero. The protagonist is no longer self-reflective and neither he nor any character invested with authority significantly attempts to evaluate or interpret the action of the film. The narrative is relatively neutral. Instead the film's discourse (camera movement, landscape, music) contains, defines, and determines our response to and evaluation of events, Barry's rise in class, alienation, and fall. The discourse is often ironic and analytic in the early part of the film; however, it functions differently in the latter part where it engages our sympathy, defining value and affirming meaning.

To be specific: in the first half of *Barry Lyndon,* long reverse zoom shots distance us from the action and from the characters who are embalmed in the landscape and the pageantry, with the music often being an additional source of ironic perspective. For example, Barry's foolish youthful romance is rendered ironic in images that are accompanied by lyrical music that is too beautiful for what is being portrayed; his duel with his rival is distanced by a reverse zoom and kept in the background, so that the costumed figures become part of the landscape. Potentially passionate events are revealed by the discourse to be comic theatrical ritual. The European wars are rendered absurd in painterly costumed tableaux, accompanied by insistent military marches. The discourse engulfs and overdetermines the minimalist narrative, situating it for evaluation, drawing it, in a sense, into the background. In the latter part of the film, however, close-ups and middle distance shots predominate, drawing us closer to Barry, establishing a sympathy that is not at first apparent in the progress of the surface of the narrative, a sympathy further expressed by the mournful music that accompanies the images. The final duel is set in a confining environment and defined by a hypotactic montage of middle-distance shots, tragic music, and sympathetic close-ups of Barry's face. He departs from the film maimed, ruined, and still uncomprehending, without having shared any of the ironic perspective which the discourse has imparted to us. However, the simple image of Barry (his back to us) entering a coach is invested with empathy and pathos by the music. The discourse has led us to both criticize and empathize with a figure who is a type of modern social mobility and alienation.

In Ermanno Olmi's recent film, *The Tree of Wooden Clogs*, the discourse is of the third kind, functioning in a rather more limited, traditional way to complete and amplify the narrative. The film is based upon historical sources. The narrative is extremely simple. A peasant chops down a tree to carve clogs for his son so that the child can walk to school; in time, the theft is discovered by the landowner; the peasant is turned off the land and departs with his family for the city. There is hardly any suspense or development of the plot; consequently the audience is not held by the unfolding of the story. The actors are nonprofessionals (peasants from the region in which the film is set), imparting an aura of authenticity to the narrative but lacking the technical resources with which to heighten the implications of the narrative by their performances.

In Olmi's film, it is the discourse which heightens and amplifies the implications of the narrative and arouses empathy. The simple elements of the plot are contained in a magnificent landscape, situated in the demanding but beautiful rhythms of nature. A few historical references (we briefly travel from the country provinces to a modern locale—electricity, fashionable clothes, a demonstration, the police) situate the lives of the peasants in a larger perspective: a way of life is passing, the peasants will be displaced to the cities, to a more alienating form of oppression in the factories. There are several extraordinary moments in which the fable is underscored by music from Bach. The images become privileged, a sublime intersection of life and interpretation, of mimesis and perspective in Auerbach's sense.[16]

Containing discourse functions not only in film but may emerge in genres of modern literature in which there is perspective but where the author is self-effacing; in so doing he adopts a position somewhat analogous to a director or *auteur* of a film who, although effaced, has control of the script, camera, and editing. In a sense, the author produces and directs the work of fiction, in which meaning is implicit, emerging from the orchestration and editing of scenes and from the montage of events and semiological background material. In the absence of a dominant authorial point of view (or of an authorial point of view that invests a central character with reliable consciousness and authority), meaning or perspective emerges from the structure and tone of the material and from a nexus of cultural and historical allusions. Thus containing discourse is often primary.[17] The mode is in some aspects both modernist and cinematic. It is of interest that Joyce opened one of the first cinemas in Dublin, as his *Ulysses* is one of the most ambitious examples of this kind of work. The fiction of William Faulkner and William Burroughs[18] also comes to mind as well as a number of major works of modernist poetry, for example, by T. S. Eliot and Ezra Pound.[19] However, John Dos Passos' novel, *USA*, may be the most overtly cinematic example.[20]

Dos Passos contains the fifty-one narratives of his *USA* trilogy in a discourse of "Newsreels," "Camera Eyes," and "Biographies" (documentary-like portraits of historical figures). The narratives are written in a minimalist metonymic style. Jean-Paul Sartre has shrewdly observed that there he does "everything possible to make his novel a mere reflection ... to show us this world, our own—to *show* it only, without explanations or comments."[21] However, unlike many of his modernist contemporaries, Dos Passos opts to contain his characters' and narrators' subjective or fragmented visions within a larger historical perspective. The "Newsreels," "Camera Eyes," and "Biographies" provide historical and cultural background, contain the narratives, and at times intersect with and transform them; for example, the concluding sections of *USA*, the apocalyptic Sacco and Vanzetti episodes that are set in the late 1920s shortly before the Depression. There the militant "all right we are two nations/America we stand defeated" discourse (conveyed by newspaper accounts of Sacco and Vanzetti's trial and execution, by snatches of poems and songs and accounts of demonstrations that took place on the day of their death, and by the historical sweep of the "Camera Eye" which places the events in a typology that extends from Christ through the Pilgrims to the present) intersects with and transforms the experience of the characters in the narrative sections and defines the reader's response to an evaluation of the text.

In the final sense, the montage configuration of "Newsreels," "Camera Eyes," and "Biographies" provides a rhetorical context for and thus structures the meaning of the paratactic progression of Dos Passos' narratives, defining our interpretation of the text. The process is somewhat more radical than in Strick's film of *Portrait of the Artist,* but the structure is similar: the subjective experience of the characters is evaluated in relation to a containing discourse, a discourse that reflects a historical description of culture and society. We may say that certain concerns of realism are thus asserted in relation to a modernist configuration.

In discussing literature, drama, and film in *The Modes of Modern Writing,* David Lodge has observed that "the most representative modernist writers (e.g. Joyce, Woolf, Stein) in their pursuit of what they took to be the real found it necessary to distort the form of their discourse until it bore less and less resemblance to the historical description of reality—which ... proves the principal nonliterary model for literary realism."[22] Strick's film of Joyce's novel can be considered a critique of this kind of distortion and an indication that a historical description of reality and standards of value associated with traditional realism may be brought to bear upon experience that is presented in modernist or minimalist narrative form. Kubrick's and Olmi's films and Dos Passos' novel are similar kinds of achievements; however they may otherwise differ, their significance is rendered by the containing discourse. Different as the forms of literature and cinema may be, the range of art as a humanist activity is extended when inner experience and outer reality are brought into relation.

*Rutgers University*

## NOTES

[1] Michel Foucault, *Language, Counter-Memory, Practice*, trans. Donald Bouchard (Ithaca: Cornell Univ. Press, 1977), p. 92.

[2] In "Fantasia of the Library" and "What is an Author?" (pp. 87-139), Foucault examines language as a "perilous limit" on what we know and what we are. Art is a series of signs and texts that primarily refer to other signs and texts, according to Foucault.

[3] Dorothy Van Ghent, "On *A Portrait of the Artist as a Young Man*," in *The English Novel: Form and Function* (New York: Holt, Rinehart and Winston, 1953), p. 263.

[4] James Joyce, *A Portrait of the Artist as a Young Man*, ed. Chester B. Anderson and Richard Ellmann (New York: Viking, 1964), pp. 252, 251. Page numbers will subsequently be cited in the text.

[5] Conversation with the author.

[6] The images are iconic, a fusion of fact and meaning. At the same time we are aware that the Irish code of Strick's discourse strives to tap our traditional responses to Dublin, the Irish landscape, Irish folk music.

[7] Harry Levin, *James Joyce: A Critical Introduction* (New York: New Directions, 1960), p. 53.

[8] Robert Scholes, "Narration and Narrativity in Film," *Quarterly Review of Film Studies*, 1 (1976), 283-97.

[9] In a sense this is a starting point for any dynamic theory of film.

[10] André Bazin, "The Evolution of the Language of the Cinema," in *What is Cinema?* ed. and trans. Hugh Gray (Berkeley: Univ. of California Press, 1967), pp. 23-40.

[11] Béla Balázs, *Theory of the Film: Character and Growth of a New Art*, trans. Edith Bone (1952; rpt. New York: Dover, 1970), p. 60.

[12] George Bluestone, "The Limits of the Novel and the Limits of the Film," in *Novels into Film* (1957; rpt. Berkeley: Univ. of California Press, 1968), esp. pp. 20-28.

[13] Sergei Eisenstein, *Film Form: Essays in Film Theory*, ed. and trans. Jay Leyda (New York: Harcourt, Brace, 1949) and *The Film Sense*, ed. and trans. Jay Leyda (New York: Harcourt, Brace, 1942, 1947).

[14] Bazin, pp. 34-38.

[15] Yet the background can interact with the foreground. For a discussion of the rhetorical complexity of the musical background at the conclusion of a significant film narrative see my "Literary Sophistication of François Truffaut," in *Film Comment*, 3, No. 3 (1965), 24-29. Rpt. in *Film And/As Literature*, ed. John Harrington (Englewood Cliffs, N.J.: Prentice-Hall, 1977).

[16] Erich Auerbach, *Mimesis*, trans. Willard Trask (New York: Anchor, 1957). It is not unlike the sort of double perspective that Auerbach found most clearly realized in Dante: surface reality intersecting with a larger perspective (spiritual, mythic, or historical).

[17] I have expanded upon this in the concluding part of "The Apocalyptic Configuration: A Stylistic Study of *Piers Plowman* in Relation to Modern Art and Literature," Diss. Sussex 1975.

[18] For a study of this aspect of Faulkner see Bruce Kawin, *Faulkner and Film* (New York: Ungar, 1977). Burroughs is more overtly cinematic but less accessible. His fold-in or montage novels incorporate a number of cinematic allusions and at times transpose themselves directly into film scripts. Their frame of reference is, however, cryptic.

[19] Pound's *Cantos*, Eliot's *The Wasteland*, much of Mayakovsky's work, Ginsberg's *Howl*, and Brown's "The Return of the Repressed" are encyclopedic montage poems, configurations of cultural and historical signs that are organized by a containing discourse (an apocalyptic vision).

[20] In Dos Passos' case there is evidence of conscious influence by film techniques apart from his brief experience as a scriptwriter. See, for example, Edward Murray, "John Dos Passos and the Camera Eye," in *The Cinematic Imagination: Writers and the Motion Pictures* (New York: Ungar, 1972), pp. 168-79.

[21] Jean-Paul Sartre, "John Dos Passos and *1919*," rpt. in *Literary Essays*, trans. Annette Michelson (New York: Philosophic Library, 1957), pp. 88-96.

[22] David Lodge, *The Modes of Modern Writing: Metaphor, Metonomy, and the Typology of Modern Literature* (Ithaca: Cornell Univ. Press, 1977), p. 46.

# Narrative Discourse in Film and Fiction: The Question of the Present Tense

### JOAN DAGLE

There is a widespread notion in film criticism that the basic difference between film and fictional narrative concerns the concept of tense: film, we are often told, can only speak in the present tense unlike written narrative which has all tenses at its disposal.[1] This assumed difference rests on the argument that any visual image isolated from its contextual situation necessarily expresses only a present reality; there is nothing in the image itself that can identify it as prior to or subsequent to any other visual image. Only a contextual reading (a character who appears older in one image than in another, a building which is more weatherbeaten, a change in the lighting) or the presence of certain conventional signals (for example, a dissolve indicating a flashback) can supply an additional tense to the grammar of film narrative. Alain Robbe-Grillet asserted this timelessness of the film image and the concomitant absence of cause and effect relationships in his defense of *Last Year at Marienbad* as merely embodying the inherent nature of all film narrative.[2]

Another variation of this argument concerns the relationship between space and time in film and fiction. Space, it is argued, is the mode of film, while time is the mode of the novel. The spatial dimension is dominant in film because time can be taken for granted; time must necessarily pass since mechanically the images must unroll sequentially. The temporal dimension is dominant in the novel because space can be taken for granted; the words must necessarily be deployed on the page.[3] Furthermore, since rendering objects in space is the mode of film, this line of reasoning asserts that film's chief difficulty lies in rendering the conceptual (the novel's forte), while the novel's chief difficulty lies in rendering the physical (film's forte). Put more simply, "film cannot render thought"[4] precisely because it so forcefully presents the physical in the present.

This impulse to see the film image as a present-tense image is also heightened by the notion of that image as irretrievable. Film images become associated with the transient and the immediate because of the technology of their presentation, one image immediately becoming lost and replaced, always receding. The difference between the act of reading and the act of viewing is acute, for re-viewing is much more problematic in film. One can certainly see a film more than once, but the opportunity to rearrange the narrative (to read ahead, to reread certain passages before continuing, to omit sections) is rare and quite apart from the ordinary process of viewing a film. The playfulness of an eighteenth-century narrator's "the reader will be pleased to remember" (which invariably sends us back to check) is not possible, nor are the more elaborate invitations to rearrange the narrative in contemporary fiction. This tyranny of the projector and attendant irretrievability of the image limit the experience of the film narrative to that relentless succession of immediate presentations and losses.

There are several aspects of what I shall call the doctrine of the present tense which need to be scrutinized more closely. In statements asserting the present-tense nature of film narrative, there is often an initial failure to distinguish the temporal structure of the act of viewing a film from the temporal structure of what is viewed; the two are treated as equivalent. The effect is to exaggerate the claim for the difference between film and fiction by omitting from the argument any consideration of the temporal structure of the act of reading a narrative. The irretrievability of the film image and the dependency on projection time may indeed heighten the sense of a present tense; however, it is not at all clear that this is in any fundamental way different from the tense of the act of reading. To read is also to be subjected to the temporal, sequential unfolding of a series of units, each of which is present or absent at any given moment. In other words, the act of either reading or viewing a narrative must necessarily take place in the present tense. Thus any attempt to differentiate the tense of film narrative from that of fictional narrative cannot rest on an appeal to the process of encountering that narrative.[5]

When we consider the aspects of the doctrine of the present tense that deal with the narrative itself rather than with the act of perceiving the narrative, we again find statements that are accepted as self-evident but which are open to challenge. One of the most frequent arguments for the claim that the film image is always in the present tense is based on a particular definition of the film image. Robbe-Grillet, for instance, asserts that "The essential characteristic of the image is its presentness. Whereas literature has a whole gamut of grammatical tenses which makes it possible to narrate events in relation to each other, one might say that on the screen verbs are always in the present tense ... by its nature, what we see on the screen *is in the act of happening,* we are given the gesture itself, not an account of it."[6] He goes on to observe that in spite of this overwhelming presentness, viewers have no difficulty in accepting the notion of flashbacks: we easily accept the conventional signal of "a few blurry seconds" as indicating a shift to the past tense; "... the sharp focus can then be resumed for the remainder of the scene without (the viewer) being disturbed by an image which is really indistinguishable from the present action, an image which is in fact *in the present tense.*"[7] What Robbe-Grillet has done is to identify as the image those segments of film which exist on either side of the blurry seconds. However, if we characterize those blurry seconds as part of the image structure of the film, the argument collapses. It seems clear that there are no legitimate grounds for excluding them. If, for example, we examine the moments of transition in *Citizen Kane,* we find the flashbacks initiated by the superimposition, a convention akin to Robbe-Grillet's blurry seconds. As the image of Thompson and the Person (or manuscript) he interviews in the narrative present recedes, the image from Kane's past comes into focus, and for a few seconds both images are visible, superimposed. If we were to isolate the frames containing the superimposition, what would we call them if not an image? These moments are not non-images; the superimposition forms an image, an image that in this case signifies precisely the transition from present to past (and back again). It is not, as Robbe-Grillet claims, a case of two present-tense images interrupted by some sort of non-image which signals the past tense, but rather a case of an image which itself speaks the past tense. These moments of superimposition are images, and one could only argue that they too are merely present-tense images if one were to again confuse the act of viewing the narrative with the narrative viewed. We view the image of the superimposition that introduces the flashback in the present tense, but the image itself signifies both present and past events.

Someone is bound to object at this point that, even if we grant the superimposition the status of image, the two parts of the superimposition do not represent two tenses, but, as Robbe-Grillet claims, are equally present; only the conventional device of the optical printer makes us read one part as past. This argument is misleading. In written narrative, the past tense (or future tense) is indicated by a switch in verb form, by a change in the linguistic signifier that readers understand and accept as indicating a shift in tense. In film narrative, the past tense (or future tense) is indicated by a similar process; a signifier is present in the image which the viewer understands and accepts as indicating a shift in tense.[8] The difference is that what appears on the other side of the signifier in a film flashback does not continue to contain the signifier: the events of Kane's life within the flashbacks are imaged in exactly the same way as Thompson's activities. This type of flashback works by having the signifiers bracket the past tense material, and it is certainly possible to conceive of a written narrative working in the same way (dreams, for instance, are sometimes retold in the present tense even though they occurred prior to the telling). It is also possible to indicate a film flashback with a signifier such as a color shift or distorted angle that persists for the duration of the flashback. Clearly, the practice of excluding the signifier of the past tense from consideration as part of the image needs to be reexamined. If such signifiers are indeed part of the image structure of film statements, the assertion that film images and film narrative unlike written narrative can speak only in the present tense is seriously compromised.

There is another sort of film image which challenges the claim that film images can only speak in the present tense, and that is the image of writing. To show a character writing or a character reading is to show a present-tense act. To fill the screen with that-which-has-been-written is a different matter. This use of the written is an element of the cinema of Jean-Luc Godard. Toward the end of *Contempt* (*Le Mépris*) we see the letter that Camille has written to Paul. The screen is filled with the words of her letter and Godard crosscuts from the accident involving Prokosch and Camille to a moving shot over the letter that bids Paul "Adieu." The relation between the shots of the accident and of the letter is unclear; however, whether Paul is reading the letter as the accident is occurring (and there is no indication of this), or the relation is one imposed by Godard, is immaterial. The image of the words of the letter is a present-tense image only with respect to the act of viewing the film. To assert that, once context has been eliminated, all film images, including this image of the writing in Camille's letter, speak in the present tense is clearly open to challenge. The image of the letter is an image of what has been written.

However, the assertion that context can be eliminated is itself problematic. All narrative, fictional or cinematic, unfolds sequentially and thus involves contextual relations, the syntagmatic or syntactic relations between the narrative units. A film or fictional narrative may disturb, suppress, or render ambiguous the contextual relations of the story being told, as in the question of whether Paul reads Camille's letter as the accident is occurring, but the narrative discourse always establishes contextual relations: the images of the accident and Camille's letter are intercut. Context is thus a complex term and the elimination of context is a complicated proposition. At the very least we would have to ask whether the elimination of context would also render the linguistic structures of fictional narrative as present-tense structures.[9] Tense signifiers exist in the linguistic structures of fictional narrative and they exist in the image structures of film narrative, as I have argued above. In both cases, the tense signifiers may be the product of syntagmatic relations (as in verb inflection or superimposition) at the level of the individual linguistic or image structure, another complication in considering the notion of context. What is of concern here, however, is the relation between tense signifiers and the larger contextual or syntagmatic patterns of narrative. Tense signifiers are recognized as such because they are conventional; they have been established by the intertextual grammar of film and fictional narrative, and yet they can be contradicted as well as reinforced by the syntagmatic relations, the specific grammar, of an individual text. For example, on the basis of convention we might assume that an image containing a superimposition signals a flashback and be proven wrong by a deliberately unconventional use of the device. Tense signifiers may indicate the syntagmatic pattern of the story conveyed through the narrative discourse (as in the flashbacks in *Citizen Kane*), but in other cases the syntagmatic relation between narrative units may constitute the signifier of tense (as in the case of the unsignalled flashbacks in Bertolucci's *The Conformist*).

My point here, however, is that the image of Camille's letter is a past-tense image for the same reason that this letter would be seen as a past-tense structure if encountered in a fictional narrative. If *Contempt* were presented as a written narrative, we would be confronted with a letter written in the present tense but encountered as a fragment from the past. Only Camille's original act of writing the letter (if this were presented) and the act of reading the letter (Paul's act within the story, our act as the narrative's readers) could be considered present-tense actions. The letter itself, read when Camille was on her way to Rome, would be perceived obviously as already-having-been-written. This is precisely the same situation we encounter in the film. Godard's presentation of the letter and the hypothetical presentation of the letter in a written version of Godard's sequence carry the identical burden of a past tense.

In *Pierrot le fou* the case is even more apparent. When Ferdinand and

Marianne reach the south of France, Ferdinand begins to write his journal, and as the film progresses Godard devotes more time to filling the screen with Ferdinand's writing. Often the images of the journal are too brief, or the camera is too close to the page, for us to read more than a word or two. At times the image is of a hand writing and in these moments the temporal structure of the act of viewing coincides with the temporal structure of the events of the narrative; both are in the present tense. At other times we see revisions being made. One image shows us a portion of the blue writing on a page of the journal being revised with red ink. Since that page has already been written, we witness the present acting on the past. In many of these later shots of the journal, however, Godard does not cut back to a shot of Ferdinand in the act of writing. We consequently have no way of placing these images within the temporal structure of the preceding and succeeding images, and they cannot be assigned any tense within the narrative.

A crucial feature of traditional definitions of the film image, and one which contributes significantly to the present-tense doctrine, is the relation of sound to image. Film theory has been dominated by the tendency to privilege the visual image (as in the term *viewer*) and to some extent this is a reflection of the tendency of films themselves. The reasons for this supremacy of the visual over the aural elements are many, involving the legacy of the silent era, technological considerations, aesthetic biases, and perceptual conditioning. The assumption that the visual image is what constitutes the unit of meaning, or at least is the predominant determinant of meaning, in film narrative is, however, clearly inadequate. The problem again concerns a confusion of two distinct entities.

The term film image is problematic, since it is so easily equated with visual image. If the narrative unit (the statement) is composed of a succession of signifiers (images plus duration), it is apparent that the definition of the film image cannot be restricted to the visual image but must allow for whatever visual and aural signifiers comprise the unit. There is an unfortunate terminological difficulty here, but the problem is more deeply rooted. In describing a shot, we are likely to limit our description to the visual (and the shot is of course fundamentally a visual unit; sound may or may not be present, or may be post-recorded), but we might add a description of the accompanying sound. However, if we analyze only a portion of the shot, one isolated moment or the image captured in a single frame, we are faced with a difficult task with respect to aural elements. There can be no equivalent for the single frame on the sound track. Analyses of the visual and the aural must proceed along different lines. Using the single frame as the irreducible unit of film analysis (as the method of determining the signifiers of any one film moment) not only privileges the visual track but insures that the aural elements will be discounted. The narrative unit, however, must logically consist of whatever visual and sound elements (music, dialogue, narration, sound effects) are present in that unit. Thus, if one speaks of the succession of film images as producing film narrative, as Christian Metz does,[10] the term film image must be taken broadly to include the aural as well as visual signifiers; otherwise, film narrative has been reduced to visual narrative.

This role of sound as an element of film narrative, as part of the film image, is crucial, for it is the failure to look closely at sound that helps sustain the notion of film narration as present-tense narration. Sound has usually been considered subordinate to the visual image and thus has been dismissed as insignificant except as an enhancement of the realistic or expressive power of the visual image.[11] Dialogue and sound effects (the sounds of a door closing or tires squealing, for example) merely enhance realistic effects; off-screen (non-diegetic) music, voices, or other sounds aid expressive or atmospheric characteristics. The identification of the visual track as the vehicle of film narrative is strengthened by this view. Bluestone maintains that although characters may talk about the past, "At best ... sound is a secondary advantage which does not seriously threaten the primacy of the spatial image."[12] Since that spatial image is always a present-tense image for Bluestone, the tense of the entire sequence and of the narrative remains present regardless of what might be on the sound track. Metz acknowledges that verbal signifiers have become more important in modern cinema, but then asserts that modern cinema "does not talk more, and the image has in no way lost its importance."[13] Although it is not likely that Metz would overlook verbal signifiers as elements of the narrative unit in film, this statement indicates that he too looks to the visual image as the primary element in the production of film narrative.

The primacy of the visual image, however, is not a self-evident, necessary condition of film narrative. There are at least two narrative situations in film which challenge this presumed privileged status of the visual image. The first is when visual image and sound do not correspond. In Orson Welles's *Touch of Evil,* such non-correspondence is a dominant feature of the narrative. In the interrogation sequence, when Quinlan questions Sanchez in the motel room, the camera follows Vargas into the bathroom and we watch as he discovers that Quinlan and his men have planted evidence to frame Sanchez, while we listen to the sound track of the interrogation in the bedroom. The tension is acute for the audience. Its attention is deliberately split between visual image and sound track, and this tension is heightened and made explicit by our inability to hear the dialogue clearly. In François Truffaut's *Two English Girls* (*Les Deux Anglaises et le Continent*), the narrator (Truffaut) at certain moments tells us about the characters, while we watch images of those characters engaged in actions or gestures which do not correspond precisely to what the narrator is describing. Again, sound is not merely enhancing or serving the visual image; the dual progression of sound and visual image convey the narrative.

The second situation which challenges the privileged status of the visual image is more extreme and involves the suppression of the visual image. This occurs in Godard's *Le Gai Savoir,* where, in addition to moments of non-correspondence between visual image and sound and moments of different sets of verbal and aural signifiers presented simultaneously, Godard eliminates the visual image entirely. We watch nothing for several minutes: the narrative is conveyed by the sound track juxtaposed with the absence of images on the visual track. Although such a situation is admittedly rare and exists for only part of a film, it confronts us nevertheless with a narrative that for at least a time is conducted solely on the sound track; and a narrative conducted on the sound track can express itself in *any of the tenses available to written narrative.*

Once we have acknowledged that sound does not always exist as an accompaniment to the visual image and that it can play a significant role in the production of film narrative, we can see several ways in which film narrative can convey a past tense through sound. Off-screen narration, for example, is a special instance of the non-correspondence of sound and visual image that can be used to directly confront the viewer/listener with a sense of pastness. What is spoken in films is heard by the listener in the present tense; however, the words themselves may speak of the past exactly as written narrative does. The first words we hear in *Two English Girls* are spoken off-screen by Claude. He tells us that "Last night I relived our story," that "someday I will write it," and that Muriel thinks "the account of our difficulties might help others." The effect of Claude's words is to cast a general retrospective aura over the story that is about to unfold, making us feel as if the narrative were written in the past tense. Since Claude tells us that someday he will write the story, we immediately wonder if what we are about to see and hear is that account. Since the first we see of Claude is his fall from the tree, followed by Anne's visit to his mother and the beginning of the story of Anne, Muriel, and Claude, we are confronted with the difficulty of placing those words. When did last night occur? The epilogue brings us to fifteen years after Claude and Muriel part but there is still no return to Claude as an off-screen narrator. The opening words remain suspended.

In Godard's *Pierrot le fou* there is a sequence involving off-screen narration which also deliberately undermines our sense of the temporal scheme of the narrative. Godard presents us with various versions of Ferdinand and Marianne's escape from her Paris apartment. Visually, the sequence appears to be structured from jump-cuts, from various scenarios depicting their method of leaving which have been jumbled together, but in a voice-over, we hear the characters say, "Marianne tells Ferdinand a story (all mixed up)."[14] We realize that Godard is presenting us with a narrative exercise, an exercise in tense that not only destroys conventional editing continuity but that leaves us with an indeterminate, or absent, temporal sequence for this portion of the narrative. In *"Pierrot* my friend" Godard writes that "two shots which follow each other do not necessarily follow each other. The same goes for two shots which do not follow each other."[15] Narrative sequence and causality (shots that follow each other) necessarily imply present/past relationships; the sequence from *Pierrot le fou* cannot be understood without the notion of more than one tense in film narrative.

The doctrine of the present tense also rests on the assumption that the relation between the filmed object and the actual object is different than the relation between other representations and their objects. Film reproduces reality in a way that literature or painting, for example, cannot. In part, of course, this assumption is justified, for the relation between the linguistic signifiers and the things to which they refer is fundamentally different from the relation between film signifiers and the things to which they refer. A film image of a tree corresponds to the actual tree that was filmed in a way that the word *tree* does not, and the physical reality of that tree has been reproduced in the image in a way that it has not in the word. This deployment of objects in space, the reproduction of physical reality, is seen as contributing to the present-tense mode because that physical presence or concreteness of the object is so immediate.

The argument for the correspondence between the filmed object and the actual object, however, for the transparency of the screen as André Bazin formulated it,[16] can be challenged. A filmed object does indeed appear to have a less arbitrary and more motivated relation to the actual object than a linguistic sign does; nevertheless a filmed object is always a framed object and thus cannot be in a natural state. The cinematic codes necessarily transform the actual object into an image, or artificial object. Reality has not been reproduced in the film image, but merely represented in a way we judge to be more accurate than in other representational systems. However, even in the images filmed with the most realistic style, distortions occur. The camera does not see in the same way that the eye does: space and depth perceptions are changed; the frame itself has imposed compositional elements on the image; the lighting and color codes have added significations not present in the actual object. In the case of film *narrative,* the correspondence between the filmed object and the actual object is further challenged. The objects or events presented in film narrative, as Metz states, are *unrealized* by the process of narrative itself.[17] To impose a beginning and an end and a discourse on the events, as all narrative does regardless of the nature of the story, is to produce a fundamental distancing effect. Narrative cannot render events naturally, but only as narrated events; thus the events are subjected to effects which distance them from the actual objects and unrealize the narrative. Recuperation can never be complete.

Although framing and distancing, necessary results of film narrative, undermine the assumption that film and its audience cannot escape the immediate presentation of physical reality, the notion persists that the presentation of the physical in film causes film narrative to have difficulty rendering the conceptual. This insistence on film as the vehicle for the physical rather than the conceptual is an important element in the doctrine of the present tense. The extreme formulation of film as presenting the physical is offered by Bluestone when he argues that film can lead us to infer thought, but "it cannot show us thought directly. It can show us characters thinking, feeling, and speaking, but it cannot show us their thoughts and feelings."[18] By denying that film narrative can show us thoughts and feelings, Bluestone is in effect asserting the present-tense doctrine, for he is claiming that film has no way of depicting what a character is thinking or has thought and must instead project only images of the act of thinking, feeling, or speaking: that is, present-tense images. The difficulty with accepting this characterization of film is that it rests on a naive view of written narrative. Can the novel actually reveal thoughts and feelings directly? Everything in the novel must be presented through written language, and it is problematic to assume that thought or feeling can be faithfully represented in written language. A narrator or a character can tell us what is felt or thought, but that is not the same as a direct presentation of feeling or thought. A narrator or a character can also describe gestures or expressions meant to convey feeling or thought, as film can show those gestures or expressions directly, but gestures and expressions are merely signs of feelings or thoughts, not the actual feelings or thoughts. Even in stream-of-consciousness narration, developed precisely as a method for approximating patterns of thought, there is a necessary formalization or stylization. If we challenge the assumption about written narrative that lies behind Bluestone's statement, we realize that certain narrative expressions of thought and feeling in film are not significantly different from those in the novel and that their similarity extends to the question of narrative tense.

*Two English Girls* presents several devices for conveying the characters' thoughts and feelings. In addition to the narrator, traditional dialogue and monologue scenes, and the initial moment of first-person narration by Claude, Truffaut gives us shots of the characters reciting passages from letters that they have previously written. After their stay in the country, Claude receives a letter from Anne in which she tells him that "You're more real to me than my sculpture," and suddenly Truffaut cuts to a close-up of Anne speaking the words of the letter. Anne is not reading the letter; the shot is strangely disembodied, devoid of background detail; the actress's gaze is fixed on a point to the side of the camera. We cannot account for such a shot within the temporal scheme of the narrative. We do not see Anne compose the letter, nor are we merely hearing her voice as Claude reads it. Truffaut forces us to contemplate Anne's face rather than remain within the temporal scheme as Claude reads the letter, making this a moment devoted to the presentation of Anne's thoughts and feelings. The same device is used later when Muriel sends her confession to Claude. Claude receives Muriel's letter and diary, and then we see Muriel as she, like Anne, speaks the words of the letter. As she narrates her sexual experience with a childhood friend, we are given the flashback images of the two young girls. Here, the past comes to us directly from Muriel; what we see is not Claude imagining the scenes as he reads Muriel's description, but Muriel remembering them. As Muriel and Anne speak in these sequences, we are confronted directly with the characters' expression of their thoughts and feelings, as directly as written narrative presents them, and in that presentation we encounter a flexible use of tense by film narrative.

The assumption that film narrative can speak only in the present tense because film images, unlike the representational system of fiction, are so tied to the physical they cannot escape the sense of their immediacy (and immediate loss) is thus misleading. I have argued above that one cannot confuse the irretrievability of the image with respect to the act of perceiving the film with an assumption that the narrative itself must be always a present-tense narrative. The act of reading a narrative is also a present-tense act and yet we readily grant that the written narrative can express the past. Both cinematic and written narrative can be seen as always speaking in the past tense since a reader encounters only that-which-has-been written and the viewer is always experiencing that-which-has-been filmed. All narrative unfolds in the present tense of the perceiver, while all written and filmed narrative is in itself a past discourse, capable of expressing more than one tense through the use of various conventional signals. In film narrative, conventions involving both visual and aural signifiers of the types I have discussed are used to indicate a variety of tenses and temporal structures. It makes little sense to argue that film narrative offers uniformly present-tense images if one ignores the tense signifiers, but that fictional narrative offers a range of tenses because of its tense signifiers.

The present-tense doctrine of film narrative is enacted in Alain Resnais' *Last Year at Marienbad*, written by Robbe-Grillet. *Marienbad* takes as its starting point Robbe-Grillet's assertion that film can only speak in one tense and then demonstrates what a film narrative limited to one tense would be like. The empty forms of *Marienbad*, the characters, A, X, and M who have no past and no fixed relations with each other and the indeterminate setting and temporal processes, provoke endless attempts by the audience, by Resnais, and even by Robbe-Grillet to supply content. *Marienbad* is a film that looks beautifully constructed and yet the narrative can barely be sustained from shot to shot or at times even within the mise-en-scène. *Marienbad* renders only the present tense, with X never able to articulate or reach the past and never able to convince A that the past existed. Narrative itself, including the investigation of the characters' psychologies that is so much a part of the novelistic inheritance, seems to be denied. Instead the audience is given only narrative traces and strange references to games and other puzzles (such as the statue of a man and woman whose story A and X attempt to supply until M stops their storytelling by offering them an authoritative answer) out of which it must attempt to construct an interpretation.

The film begins as the camera tracks through the incredibly ornate corridors of the building while X, off-screen, speaks: "Once again—I walk on, once again, down these corridors, through these halls, these galleries, in this structure—of another century, this enormous, luxurious, baroque, lugubrious hotel—where corridors succeed endless corridors—silent deserted corridors overloaded with a dim, cold ornamentation of woodwork, stucco, moldings, marble, black mirrors, dark paintings, columns, heavy hangings...."[19] X's opening narration (of which this is only a fragment) deliberately evokes the image of this hotel as a labyrinth of endless corridors, but it also suggests that the past, that other century of which this hotel is a trace, is labyrinthian, made up of those endless, deserted corridors which have become burdened with the overload of detailed ornamentation; the past is empty, dead, but encrusted with the accumulation of content and meaning. There is also the implication of the corridors, and the past, leading back to the same corridors until present and past become meaningless distinctions. X's narration takes us into this labyrinth of tense. "Once again—I walk on" describes the immediate present while implying the continuation of the action, the repetition of the past.

What we see in this sequence appears to be so overwhelmingly immediate in part because of the way it is shot. The tracking movement of the camera seems to correspond to or reinforce the movement of the film through the projector, so that the duration of the film (the present-tense act of viewing) becomes identified with the tense of the material shown. The use of movement in the opening of *Marienbad* is deliberately abstract (we see the ceilings, tops of doorways, occasionally walls) in order to heighten this creation of a timeless present.[20] Camera movement renders the physical reality of the images immediately present, as opposed to the still photograph which strongly suggests the past nature of the objects in the frame. The tension throughout *Marienbad* between the tracking camera and the frequent arrangement of the characters in frozen, statue-like groups within the mise-en-scène suggests the same ambiguous and indeterminate relation between past and present as X's opening narration.

The "timeless present" which eventually triumphs in *Marienbad* is based on the elimination of tense. The relationship between past and present, memory and reality, is so disturbed and ambiguous the only real (or verifiable) temporal order remaining is the duration of X's narration, the duration of the narrative and the viewing/listening act. *Marienbad* thus demonstrates the doctrine of the present tense, but it is crucial to recognize that it does so precisely because it eliminates or subverts certain conventional signifiers of narrative discourse in film. We watch A, dressed in black, move toward the camera through a frozen group of characters; then there is what appears to be a continuity cut, but we see her, dressed in a light-colored brocade, from behind as she ascends the staircase and says, "Tell me the rest of our story." These succeeding shots make it clear that in Godard's words, we cannot assume that one shot which follows another follows another. X, off-screen, describes A conversing with a group of friends, but we see her alone, outside, moving through the grounds in slow motion. Shortly after, we see X and M at one of the card tables, but X's narration describes the episode of the broken heel of A's shoe. We eventually realize, or are invited to assume, that the slow-motion shot of A moving through the grounds comes from the sequence in which she breaks the heel of her shoe, but it does not come from this sequence in any recognizable way. We merely have an image of A, dressed and moving in a certain way, that appears to correspond to another image of A similarly dressed and moving which shows her break the heel of her shoe. Any necessary connection between the two images, however, is suppressed. By suppressing the signifiers which establish temporal relations within shots or sequences, *Last Year at Marienbad* shows how film images (visual image and sound) articulate tenses. The timeless present of *Marienbad* reveals that film narrative can speak entirely in the present tense only with great difficulty.

*Rhode Island College*

## NOTES

[1] "The novel has three tenses; the film has only one. From this follows almost everything else one can say about time in both media." George Bluestone, *Novels into Film* (1957; rpt. Berkeley: Univ. of California Press, 1968), p. 48. There are echoes of Bluestone's analysis of tense in film and fiction in many textbooks on film, for example in John Fell, *Film: An Introduction* (New York: Praeger, 1975), pp. 78-79; and numerous critical articles make reference to the present-tense nature of film narrative, for example Susan Sontag's "Godard" in *Styles of Radical Will* (New York: Farrar, Strauss, 1969), p. 157. Alain Robbe-Grillet also argued for this distinction in tense between film and the novel in his introduction to the movie script, *Last Year at Marienbad,* trans. Richard Howard (New York: Grove, 1962), p. 12.

[2] Robbe-Grillet, pp. 7-15.

[3] See Bluestone, Ch. 1, "Of Time and Space," p. 61; Robert Scholes, "Narration and Narrativity in Film," *Quarterly Review of Film Studies* (1976), rpt. in *Film Theory and Criticism*, ed. Gerald Mast and Marshall Cohen, 2nd ed. (New York: Oxford Univ. Press, 1979), pp. 417-33. Citations are from this edition.

[4] Bluestone, pp. 47-48; for the argument in the preceding sentence, see Scholes, pp. 427-28, 432-33.

[5] The issue of irretrievability is itself problematic since the notion rests on the conventional (albeit virtually universal) means of projection. Theoretically at least it is possible to envision means of projection that would allow for the same processes of rearranging the film narrative as written narratives afford; the development of video discs and the like, for instance, holds the potential for radically altering viewing methods.

[6] Robbe-Grillet, p. 12.

[7] Robbe-Grillet, pp. 12-13.

[8] Part of the difficulty is with equating linguistic structures and the structures of the language of film. Verb inflections and superimpositions are not equivalent (language systems and the system of film language are not equivalent systems). However, in both cases, understanding that the past tense has been indicated depends on some understanding of context or of the syntagmatic relations. For example, a hasty glance at a sentence could cause one to mistake *lead* (noun) for *lead* (verb) or *have* (present tense) for *have* (auxiliary verb in past tense), just as the superimposition can indicate things other than flashbacks.

[9] Contextual relations exist in all narrative discourse. There are also the contextual relations of the story's events or segments and the possibility that contextual (syntagmatic) relations exist within the individual sign: adding "-ed" to a verb form; combining two images to produce the image of superimposition. (This latter is clearly not what the critics I argue against meant by context).

[10] Christian Metz, *Film Language: A Semiotics of the Cinema*, trans. Michael Taylor (New York: Oxford Univ. Press, 1974), pp. 17-19.

[11] The tendency to treat sound as an accompaniment or enhancement of the visual is demonstrated in numerous film textbooks. See, for example, Louis D. Giannetti, *Understanding Movies*, 2nd ed. (Englewood Cliffs, N.J.: Prentice-Hall, 1976), pp. 270-71, 183-222. One of the most influential works which argues for the subordination of sound to visual image is Erwin Panofsky's "Style and Medium in the Motion Pictures" (1934), rpt. in Mast and Cohen, pp. 237-63. Panofsky argues for the wisdom of the term "moving picture" and develops his "principle of coexpressibility" (pp. 245, 249) according to which sound has an accompanying function to visual spectacle.

[12] Bluestone, p. 57.

[13] Metz, p. 189.

[14] This sequence recalls the frequently reported debate between Godard and Georges Franju. " 'But surely, Monsieur Godard,' the exasperated Franju is reported to have said, 'you do at least acknowledge the necessity of having a beginning, middle, and end in your films.' 'Certainly,' Godard replies, 'But not necessarily in that order' " (Sontag, p. 157).

[15] Jean-Luc Godard, "*Pierrot* my friend," *Cahiers du Cinema*, 171 (1965), rpt. in *Godard on Godard*, ed. Jean Narboni and Tom Milne and trans. Tom Milne (New York: Viking, 1972), p. 215.

[16] See André Bazin, "The Ontology of the Photographic Image," *What Is Cinema?* ed. and trans. Hugh Gray (Berkeley: Univ. of California Press, 1967) and "The French Renoir," *Jean Renoir*, ed. François Truffaut and trans. W. W. Halsey II and William H. Simons (New York: Dell, 1971).

[17] Metz, "A closed discourse ... proceeds by unrealizing a temporal sequence of events" (p. 28).

[18] Bluestone, p. 48.

[19] Robbe-Grillet, p. 18.

[20] "There is no last year, and Marienbad is no longer to be found on any map. This

past, too, has no reality beyond the moment it is evoked with sufficient force; and when it finally triumphs, it has merely become the present, as if it had never ceased to be so" (Robbe-Grillet, p. 12). Robbe-Grillet also speaks of the images or imaginings of memory as always in the present, acting "something like an interior film continually projected in our own minds," and this leads him to equate the processes of cinema with mental processes until he arrives at the inevitable, and unfortunate, phrase "the total cinema of our mind" (p. 13).

# Audience Engagement in Wenders' *The American Friend* and Fassbinder's *Ali: Fear Eats the Soul*

PETER RUPPERT

Among the most influential critical strategies animating contemporary literary theory is the growing concern with the role of the reader and the development of various types of reader-oriented response aesthetics. Although great theoretical diversity exists among the leading practitioners of this approach,[1] their shared theoretical and critical practice constitutes an unambiguous shift in the direction of narrative analysis. Essentially this practice focuses on readers reading rather than on texts that are being read, studies literature (and film) as a form of communication rather than a self-referential activity, and views the text as a process rather than a representational object—a process in which the reader is an active participant in producing the meaning and thus concretizing the text rather than passively consuming it.

In seeking to define the relationship between reader and text, reception theories have raised complex questions about the contribution of the text—questions concerning its coherence or incoherence, the determinacy and indeterminacy of meaning, and the possibility of permanent artistic value. Opponents have asked whether this focus on the reader's role does not dissolve the text into the reader's experience. Advocates have claimed that, conversely, in formalist textual analysis it is the reader who vanishes into the text, eliminated from a communicatory process that cannot in reality exist without him. Wolfgang Iser, who has developed the philosophical foundations for the approach, stresses instead the phenomenological interplay of reader and text, a relationship grounded in the interpenetration of subject and object in all phenomenal experience.[2]

Working from these premises, Robert Scholes has suggested the word "narrativity" to designate "the process by which a perceiver actively constructs a story from the fictional data provided by any narrative medium."[3] Scholes argues that although the term is used (primarily in French criticism) to refer to a property of films, it is more descriptive of the active, creative role of the reader than of the passive role of the narrative text, whether verbal or filmic. For Scholes all forms of narration require the participation of an interpreter who is "situated in a space/time reference different from that of the events narrated," an interpreter actively engaged in "producing" the text rather than simply allowing it to print itself upon his mind. Essentially he activates or energizes the text through acts of perceiving and processing. The text generates a fiction that he perceives and recreates, guided by the narrative that activates his thoughts and emotions.

In this process the text functions as a kind of blueprint or framework that induces or promotes narrativity in the perceiver. It provides perspectives and codes that prestructure but do not entirely control the experience of narrativity. Thus the relationship between perceiver and text is primarily a reciprocal or dialectical one: the narrative, created by the author, is realized or concretized by the reader, who in turn is guided by the narrative. This view of the reader as a dialectical partner in the communicatory process does not minimize the significance of the text but instead underscores the importance of the reader's experience and competence in reading texts, since to a great extent these qualities determine the richness of the fictional world that is disclosed in any act of reading.

Different kinds of texts, Scholes points out, require different kinds of narrativity. With verbal texts, the process is to a great extent one of "translating ... verbal signs into images," of visualizing and concretizing what is described or suggested (NN, p. 286). In realizing the concrete and specific data suggested by a verbal narrative, we are guided by conceptions of the world implicit in the descriptive and expositional matrix of that narrative. Iser refers to these as "schematized aspects" of the text, conventions and organizing principles that "offer us knowledge of the conditions under which the imaginary object is to be produced" as a mental image in the reader's mind (AR, p. 137). At the same time Iser points out that a literary text leaves the reader freer than a film text does to "constitute" the text in a way that is personally meaningful, for the literary text—a linguistic rather than a visual production—"makes conceivable that which has not been formulated" (AR, p. 139).

Scholes explains the semiotic basis for the distinction being drawn here. He writes that in verbal narrative "each sign is first interpreted as a concept or category and then, where this is relevant and possible, connected to a referent of some sort." In a sense, the film narrative reverses the direction of this process, providing the reader with "a sign tightly tied to a specific referent, which [he] then may relate to a categorical concept or a set of such concepts by a process which may be partly conscious and partly not" (NN, p. 291). Thus the concreteness and specificity of the film image—the source of the particular power of the cinematic medium—might be seen in one sense to limit the range of the reader's freedom in constituting the text. Yet, as Scholes points out, the cinematic text, because it is unmediated by the detailed description and reflection provided by verbal narrative, requires this mediation in the form of viewer narrativity if the full measure of a film's power of signification is to be realized. As Scholes expresses it, "a well-made film requires interpretation while a well-made novel may only need understanding" (NN, p. 291). The film viewer's narrativity is, then, in some ways more demanding—because more "categorical and abstract"—than the narrativity required of the reader of a verbal text. It involves "the conceptualization of images and the construction of frameworks of causality and value around such concepts" (NN, p. 292).

There are, to be sure, limits of tolerance inherent in reader narrativity, whether verbal or filmic. Where a narrative is too clear, too predictable, or too obviously tendentious, narrativity is diminished or even paralyzed. The reader's intellectual and emotional processes are only minimally involved and the experience becomes boring. This occurs frequently with television narratives and with novels and films that reduce narrativity to either acceptance or rejection of the message. On the other hand, narratives can also be too obscure, too minimal, and thereby frustrate the viewer in another way. At this extreme too large a burden is placed on the viewer. Scholes points out that much of avant-garde literature and film, in trying to increase the space for narrativity, runs the risk of losing the reader altogether. The extreme forms on this side of the spectrum (empty canvasses, soundless concerts) provide only trivial possibilities for narrativity and are self-limiting in stimulating imaginative viewer participation (NN, p. 290). Both extremes destroy the interdependent and dialectical relationship between reader and text. Thus Scholes cautions makers of narratives not to deny their readers "the satisfactions of story" (NN, p. 290).

Since such satisfactions are withheld, to varying degrees, by many modern and post-modern writers and filmmakers, it is their works that provide the most dramatic illustrations of the value of reader-response criticism. Where the great majority of earlier narratives provided fully detailed and resolved plots, fixed points of valuation, and omniscient narrators to ensure the correct reader appraisal of characters, actions, and events, the ambiguous and open-ended narratives of much contemporary literature and film require the reader to fill in the openings in the text, put its parts together, and determine its significance. Writers such as Brecht, Pirandello, Ionesco, Borges, Nabokov, Frisch, and Fowles, and filmmakers including Godard, Resnais, and Antonioni have increasingly disregarded established conventions of narrative and challenged the narrativity of the reader or viewer. Primarily the tendency of such experiments in both literary and film works has been to disrupt conventional temporal and causal structures, forcing the reader or viewer out of a passive role and into an active one in constructing the essential shape and significance of texts that are fragmentary, elusive, and sometimes confounding.

Such developments have required an increasingly abstract, conceptual kind of narrativity of the reader of literary and film texts, but Scholes argues that it is particularly "the cinematic world [that] invites—even requires—conceptualization" for "the images presented to us, their arrangement and juxtapositioning, are narrational blueprints for a fiction that must be constructed by the viewer's narrativity" (NN, p. 293). This demand of film texts for an abstract, conceptual form of narrativity on the part of the viewer is well illustrated in two representative films of the New German Cinema: Wim Wenders' *The American Friend,* based on Patricia Highsmith's novel *Ripley's Game,* and R. W. Fassbinder's *Angst essen Seele auf* [sic] (*Ali: Fear Eats the Soul*), based on Douglas Sirk's *All That Heaven Allows.* These new German films exemplify two different ways in which viewer narrativity is called upon to conceptualize the images of narrative cinema, and both films seek a higher level of reflection in the viewer than do the works on which they are based.

In *The American Friend* viewer narrativity consists of translating the rich visual texture and ambiguous sequences of the film into a network of potential meaning and significance. Wenders uses Highsmith's novel primarily as a framework upon which to build his own more complex story, one concerned with the recognitions and conflicts of an individual put into the extreme situation or confronting his own imminent death. This situation, known well to readers of existentialist literature, requires rendering the experiences of anxiety (in the face of extinction) and dread (at the recognition of one's responsibility for one's choice, one's life). To communicate effectively, the film must give the viewer a sense of the protagonist's thought processes as he undergoes radical transformation.

Such radical transformations are difficult to render, even in a discursive medium. The rendering of even comparatively static states of mind is considered by many film theorists to be virtually beyond the capability of film. George Bluestone, for example, has claimed that "film, having only arrangements of space to work with, cannot render thought, for the moment thought is externalized it is no longer thought."[4] But such distinctions concerning the capabilities of verbal and filmic texts do not take into consideration the undeniable role of the reader in constituting the meaning of the text. Wenders' film is able to render complex states of mind and even subtle transformations in the consciousnesses of his characters by making use of the viewer's narrativity. Instead of presenting a detailed, smoothly coherent story, Wenders impedes the flow of the narrative with gaps that must be filled in by the viewer. For example, abrupt juxtaposition of unrelated scenes forces the viewer to supply missing transitions or to devise a framework in which the scenes can be related. Disruption or fragmentation of conventional temporal or causal sequences causes these scenes to resonate with multiple possibilities for interpretation. These devices function as catalysts, generating in the viewer the same apprehension at the openness and ambiguity of the fictional world that the protagonist experiences within the world of the film. The gaps in the narrative make it possible to communicate the protagonist's experiences to the viewer's consciousness in such a way that the latter is able to comprehend the protagonist's state of mind.

These gaps give the narrative the kind of discontinuity that has led one critic to observe that "narrative plotting has never been one of Wenders' strengths" and that in his films "loose ends abound everywhere."[5] These loose ends take on positive value when they are understood as part of an attempt to accelerate viewer narrativity and increase the evocative power of the film. A brief comparison of *The American Friend* with *Ripley's Game* will demonstrate how evocative film can be in stimulating narrativity, for in this case the film mobilizes the viewer's imaginative and conceptual capabilities far more effectively and discloses states of consciousness more palpably than the novel does.

*Ripley's Game* is a psychological thriller that makes few demands on its reader. The narrative recounts in clearly linked chronological sequences the events that lead to a bizarre friendship between an American expatriate, Tom Ripley, and an English picture framer, Jonathan Trevanny, and to the latter's death. The narrative begins with Ripley's offer to help a friend who needs someone "above reproach" to "do one or perhaps two 'simple murders.'"[6]

Ripley's criminal past (which includes murder, theft, forgery, and fencing stolen property) makes him ineligible and his present circumstances (financial well-being, a wife from a respected and wealthy French family) make him unwilling to risk his situation. He suggests an acquaintance, Jonathan Trevanny, for the job, partly to repay an insult Jonathan has directed toward him and partly as a "nasty game" to see if Jonathan, who is terminally ill with leukemia, can be corrupted by money.

In contrast to the amoral and uncommitted Ripley, Jonathan is characterized as a man of integrity. He is a gentle father, a loving husband, and a dedicated craftsman. He is also poor and expects to live only from one to six more years. Ripley's game is to spread rumors that Jonathan's condition has worsened in order to plunge him into doubt concerning the time he has left and thus to tempt him to commit murder for the money his wife and child will soon need. At first Jonathan firmly resists the offer, but doubt erodes his resolve and he agrees to commit first one murder and then another.

It is during the second murder, on a train from Munich to Paris, that the friendship between the two men is formed. Ripley comes to Jonathan's aid just as the latter loses his nerve. Motivated by a sense of responsibility for getting Jonathan into this situation, by an intense hatred for the Mafia, and by the excitement and adventure of it all, Ripley kills ruthlessly and efficiently as Jonathan ineptly stands by. The friendship thus established, the narrative develops the male bond between the two, the disruption of Jonathan's tranquil domestic life, and the gradual deterioration of his health. Ripley and Jonathan cooperate on several more murders, which are necessary since the Mafia is seeking its own revenge. The friendship ends with Jonathan's death, not through leukemia but by a bullet from a Mafia gun. His widow, who has seen Ripley commit murder, withholds this information from the police in order to keep the money Jonathan has been paid. Ripley, virtually unchanged by his friendship with Jonathan or Jonathan's death, survives to take up his former activities: gardening, painting, playing the harpsichord.

Wenders' version of the story also focuses on the friendship between Ripley (Dennis Hopper) and Jonathan (Bruno Ganz); but in the film this friendship is more ambivalent, indeed, more multivalent. The self-possessed Ripley of the novel, with his aristocratic tastes and lifestyle, is transformed in the film into the rootless, culturally disinherited, anguish-ridden Ripley who keeps a journal in the form of a cassette recorder into which he dictates: "I know less and less who I am and who anybody else is." A displaced American living in Hamburg, the Ripley of the film is a seedy, pathetic gangster permeated by angst but lacking the seriousness or insight to understand its significance. He wears a cowboy hat and lives in a mansion that resembles the White House; his house is cluttered with pool table, juke box, cassette recorder, polaroid camera, and an assortment of kitsch objects that leave no doubt about their American origin.

The Ripley of the film is simultaneously reminiscent of the protagonists of gangster films (loners often invested with pathos), westerns (outlaws, outsiders), and caper films (free-footed adventurers looking for a game to play and a temporary bond with fellow players). He is also representative of the values of American capitalism in its most computerized, dehumanized, multi-national form. For Ripley, everything is a commodity to be bought and sold; and, as in the case of the forged paintings he fences in Europe, authenticity is not an issue. Ripley's single redeeming quality is that he seems to realize the truth about himself. It is his recognition that he knows "less and less" who he is and who "anybody else is" that draws him to Jonathan, an individual who knows very well who he is and who lives authentically in this knowledge.

A Swiss craftsman now living in Hamburg, Jonathan is morally and culturally superior to Ripley (considerably more so than the Jonathan of the novel, who is merely a quiet, conventional man). Unlike Ripley, who defines his profession as "making money," Jonathan restores old paintings and frames them. An art dealer observes early in the film, however, that Jonathan has lost his skill as a restorer and now simply builds frames. This loss of skill is related to Jonathan's illness and is an early indication that he is losing a measure of his assurance and groundedness. Jonathan is shown in his workshop in the midst of personal objects and tools that possess the patina of use and familiarity. His home and family life are characterized by a parallel dignity and serenity, and this is contrasted with the constant motion and noise of the mechanized and anonymous surroundings of Ripley (both his tavern-like home and the New York to which he returns several times during the film).

These metonymically suggestive cultural contrasts invite the viewer to conceptualize about old and new world values and the encroaching influence of the latter. Airplanes, escalators, video monitors (which observe the first murder even though no one is watching the monitors) all suggest the pervasive and impersonal influence of American technological values. Slowly corrupted by his "American Friend" and drawn into his anonymous and violently purposeless world, Jonathan finds himself drawn to Ripley even as he is destroyed by the friendship.

In a sense it is Jonathan who knows less and less who he is. At the same time, Ripley becomes more centered, more serious through his friendship with Jonathan. He is able to transcend mere self-interest and risks his own safety to come to Jonathan's aid on the train at the time of the second murder (in the film this is not the beginning of the friendship but occurs after the two men have already changed their minds about one another and have begun to care about each other). Nor is the friendship without redeeming significance for Jonathan. He seems to find in Ripley something that neither his wife nor his child can provide: perhaps a sense of dread, a fear of nothingness, to match his own and thus a way to come fully into contact with the reality of his condition. Similarly, the implicit cultural criticism that we recognize in the film comes up against the subtler recognition that this corrupt setting is simply the context in which the contemporary individual must make his life choices, and not an excuse, or even an explanation, for those choices. Almost all the encounters of the film have both these positive and negative charges, confronting the viewer with an ambiguity that he is left to resolve, or to accept.

The viewer's narrativity plays an even greater role in comprehending Jonathan's gradual transformation from a passive, gentle man to a murderer, a transformation conveyed almost palpably by the film's discontinuous, fragmentary, highly elusive narrative. These qualities of the narrative demand an attentive and ultimately a highly conceptual kind of narrativity from the viewer. Following these discontinuous events closely at the level of felt experience, the viewer shares Jonathan's disorientation at the unpredictable and increasingly bizarre nature of his experiences and, like Jonathan, struggles to make sense of them on the conceptual level. Wenders accomplishes this close emotional and conceptual involvement of the reader in the text through an intense and extensive employment of what Iser has called "blanks" in the text.

In *The Act of Reading* Iser distinguishes between "two basic structures of indeterminacy in the text—blanks and negations" (*AR*, p. 182). The blank functions as a basic condition for communication and constitutes a "basic element of the interaction between text and reader." For Iser the blank "designates a vacancy in the overall system of the text, the filling in of which brings about an interaction of textual patterns" (*AR*, p. 182). Thus blanks (or gaps) separate segments of the narrative that must be connected by the reader/viewer. They "denote what is absent from the text and can only be supplied by the reader's ideational activity" (*AR*, p. 216). The linking of segments, then, is not formulated by the text but is essential to producing the text and is the province of the reader. It is here that narrativity takes place. Iser goes on to define how, by obstructing or impeding the process of fluid narrative construction, blanks promote narrativity on a higher, more complex level. Wenders' film uses the kind of blanks that Iser defines as missing links between segments, perspectives, characters, and situations to accelerate interaction between viewer and text. By suspending the smooth flow of the narrative these blanks compel greater viewer activity in establishing relationships and induce the viewer to try to reconcile discrepancies and synthesize contrasting values and viewpoints.

An illustration of this use of blanks occurs in the opening sequences of the film set in New York and Hamburg. The cutting from one to the other location is abrupt, without transition or clear designation. These sequences attempt to establish contrasts between Ripley and Jonathan, but the viewer must supply the connections and at this point he is faced with a network of possibilities. We first see Ripley in New York with a painter (Nicholas Ray) who is forging paintings of a dead painter (Derwatt). Ripley is in New York to pick up a painting that he will later sell at an auction in Hamburg, but his background and activities are still undefined. Then there is a sudden cut to Hamburg (without identification of the city) and we see Jonathan walking in the street with his small son. The contrasting images encourage the viewer to find the missing links; the withholding of information acts as a stimulus. Details slowly emerge, suggesting possible connections, but these remain provisional. The blanks in the narrative make it impossible to anticipate the characters' futures, and this creates an element of suspense.

Repeated switching of viewpoints from Jonathan to Ripley forces the viewer to construct a sense of their similarities and differences and to bring the story to life. As more and more segments come and go and the viewer sets them off against one another, the relationship takes form. In place of contrasts between the two, we begin to see Ripley and Jonathan as reciprocal reflectors. Gradually they begin to resemble one another physically. During the second murder on the train their friendship is fully realized and they appear as doubles on the screen. At the same time this resemblance is qualified by their diverse reactions to the violence on the train. Ripley goes to the dining car to order a meal; Jonathan goes to an isolated car and screams, experiencing a terrifying sense of freedom (and guilt) as he confronts the possibilities within himself.

It is the blanks in the narrative that provide space for the viewer to organize, reflect upon, and complete a mesh of connections only suggested by the film narrative. Rather than simply internalizing the text, he is actively engaged in constructing it, transforming the segments by making them act upon one another. The colliding images influence and condition each other, and this collision generates meaning—not in and of itself but with the viewer's active participation. For example, Jonathan's reaction on the train prompts us, reading backwards, to see a fuller significance in an earlier scene in Paris when, about to return to Hamburg after he has successfully brought off the first murder, he experiences a sudden sense of exhiliration. This occurs as he passes a video monitor like the one that had witnessed his act. In this context, his sense of exhiliration signifies more than his relief at not being caught; it signifies his recognition of his freedom to act and to give his acts their meaning (since there has been no one else there to define this act). His contrary reaction on the train after the second murder adds a further dimension to this recognition. In a way, these two reactions become the context for one another (because the reader is able to put them together this way) and convey Jonathan's growing sense both of the duplicity of consciousness—its being able to feel more than one way about anything, even so important a thing as murder—and of the inescapability of choices. No matter what one feels about the act one has committed, one has irrevocably done it. Jonathan cries out in anguish on the train not only because of what he did in Paris (and what he has just helped to do here) but because he can react to these actions in various ways.

We are able to read these scenes this way because they occur in a context of other scenes that tend in the same direction. Jonathan's recognition of the insubstantiality of his ego (his personality, his character) grows out of his confrontation of the insubstantiality of his very existence. After he receives a letter informing him of rumors of a change in his condition, he is gripped by fear. In the montage that follows, the viewer sees Jonathan in constant motion against a background that is continually moving and shifting. He is trying to determine how much time he has left, but that time cannot be specified. For the viewer even the nature of his disease is mysterious, contributing to the text's saturation with ambiguity. His trip to the doctor, his encounter with Reeves (a stranger who asks him to commit murder), his trip to Paris to a blood specialist and into a violent underworld in which he is a stranger—all against a background of moving escalators, streetcars, subways, airplanes—continually dislocate the viewer, providing him with a sense of disorientation similar to that Jonathan experiences when he finds himself with a gun in his hand about to murder someone he doesn't know. Like Jonathan, the viewer must make some sense out of these events, find their common denominator.

Alongside these events (at first) is Jonathan's changing relationship with Ripley. At first Jonathan feels a virtually instantaneous antipathy for Ripley. The next time they meet (when Ripley comes to Jonathan's shop) Jonathan is clearly attracted to the American. They exchange small gifts. Gradually it becomes clear that Ripley is part of the larger confusion of his life, but Jonathan does not know exactly how and does not seem actually to care. As he becomes more and more involved with Ripley and the chain of events in which they act together, he experiences another aspect of his own ambiguity, his own duplicity. His friendship with Ripley and his secrecy about his recent activities alienate him from his wife and from his former self or sense of himself. Each time he returns home it is with a greater sense of alienation from this former life. Yet Wenders underscores the claim that Jonathan's past makes upon him: each return is signalled by a repetition of an establishing shot of their apartment building (each time in increasing darkness), accompanied by a haunting motif on the sound track. Once inside, Jonathan, feeling estranged, nevertheless comes upon evidence of his unbreachable connection with this life constructed out of his earlier choices. At the same time, his more recent choices cut him off from this life. He is both at home and not at home in this former life, this former self.

If we attend closely to the fragments of this narrative and to the images in which it unfolds we come to the same recognitions Jonathan comes to: that we both have and don't have identity, since we compose that identity day by day as long as we live; that we can add to the past but we cannot subtract from it; that we can look at things differently from day to day, and see things differently than others do, but that our actions remain the same, remain what they are, have their undeniable effects; that finally we can only accept responsibility for ourselves and live in the midst of contradiction, both our own and that that exists between ourselves and others; and that we can only know this fully as we come to accept the reality of death and begin to live our own temporality.

This existential framework, more or less developed and refined as the reader is more or less competent to recognize it, holds together the fragmentary narrative of *The American Friend,* but at any degree of development it is a framework that can be constructed only with the viewer's active involvement in conceptualizing the images of the text. As the common denominator for an interpretation of the film, this framework essentially consists in the denial of a common denominator in human experience. In this film that experience has all the duplicity, the complexity, the thickness of multiple signification that it possesses in life. And we recognize these qualities through the blanks in the narrative, which summon us to try to make coherent Jonathan's profoundly moving and profoundly confusing experience. To the extent that we succeed only partially, our experience as readers of this text enables us to comprehend the protagonist's experience. Thus it is ultimately its reliance on and exploitation of the viewer's narrativity that gives the film its full power and resonance.

In *The American Friend* temporal, spatial, and causal blanks in the narrative compel the viewer to connect segments, compare perspectives, weigh contrasts, and balance opposing claims. They constitute the text's "basic structure of indeterminacy" and initiate interaction between viewer and screen. *Ali: Fear Eats the Soul* relies on a second kind of blank to stimulate viewer narrativity. In distinguishing between syntagmatic and paradigmatic axes of reading, Iser discusses a second kind of blank—"negation"—which stimulates and regulates narrativity in a different way: "the function of the blanks is dual in nature: on the syntagmatic axis of reading they constitute links between the perspective segments [sic] of the text; on the paradigmatic axis they constitute the links between negated norms and the reader's relation to the text" (*AR*, p. 216). Negations, produced on the paradigmatic axis of reading, generate blanks on the content level of the text. They link "the reader's ideational activity to the answer which the text attempts to give to a specific historical or social problem" (*AR*, p. 212). Essentially, negations occur when a familiar content (collective experience, norms, shared values) is removed from its normal context and set into an unfamiliar one. Such estrangement of the familiar forces the reader to become consciously aware of norms and values he may unconsciously have taken for granted. If these norms and values are questioned or negated, the reader's own position is inevitably affected. He is stimulated to provide a new meaning or new knowledge to fill the blank left by negation. This process affects not only the reader's relationship to the text but also his relationship to his familiar world.

Negations thus function very much like the principle of estrangement first developed by the Russian Formalists (*ostranenie*) and widely known through the work of Bertolt Brecht. Brecht defined the *Verfremdungseffekt* (estrangement effect) in his *Short Organon for the Theater:* "A representation which [estranges] is one which allows us to recognize its subject, but at the same time makes it seem unfamiliar."[7] The principle implies both cognitive and creative activity on the part of the spectator: a familiar subject is made strange to make the spectator aware of its deficiencies or contradictions, a process that simultaneously opens a critical space and induces the spectator to fill the vacancy that results. Brecht's interests in stimulating narrativity were social, political, and historical. He wanted to make the spectator aware that he is not an observer of a reified world but an active agent in an open world that has been formed by men and can be transformed by men.

Fassbinder's film *Ali* stimulates viewer narrativity in a similar way by defamiliarizing a familiar world (represented through a conventional narrative) through negations that force the viewer to fill in the void created by the cancelling of expected norms and values. In order to guide viewer narrativity concerning the social and moral implications of the story, Fassbinder subverts elements of a familiar genre, Hollywood melodrama. He achieves this by utilizing various estrangement techniques such as the extensive framing of shots through windows and doorways and the recording of relentness stares (gazes) through which characters objectify each other (in turn making the spectator conscious of his own activity of objectifying); and also by leaving the narrative open-ended, forcing the viewer to speculate on the likely sequel.

Unlike Wenders' film, *Ali* has a clear, unambiguous narrative and consequently a higher "entertainment factor."[8] To summarize briefly, *Ali* relates a love story between Emmi, a German cleaning woman in her fifties, and Ali, a young Moroccan *Gastarbeiter* (immigrant worker). The two are drawn to one another through mutual loneliness. As a *Gastarbeiter,* Ali is a racial and cultural outsider. His alienation is powerfully rendered by his broken German. Emmi, a widow whose children have all moved away, is physically, economically, and socially outside the mainstream of German society. As their relationship develops into a mutually felt bond they are subjected to various kinds of hostility and prejudice from Emmi's children, neighbors, and co-workers and from Ali's friends and acquaintances. Trying at first to ignore their rejection, they soon find the pressures of disapproval, communicated by the constant stares of others, to be unbearable. To escape they go on a brief holiday. Upon their return they suddenly find themselves accepted by family, neighbors, friends. But they soon learn that basic attitudes have remained unchanged and purely economic motives of expediency and exploitation account for their acceptance: neighbors want to use Emmi's basement storage area; her son (who called her a whore when she announced her intention to marry Ali) now wants to use her for baby-sitting chores; the grocer (who previously refused to wait on Ali) now recognizes that he needs more customers if he is to compete with the new supermarket in the neighborhood.

Just when the viewer thinks that this acceptance by society (even though it is only superficial) will resolve the previous tensions, new problems begin to develop on an interpersonal level. Enjoying her reunion with family and friends, Emmi begins to objectify Ali through the projection of stereotypes. The climax of this sequence occurs in a scene in which she exhibits Ali to her friends, asks them to feel his muscles, and points out how, for a foreigner, he is clean and showers daily. When Ali abruptly leaves she points out that as a foreigner he is subject to unpredictable moods. This situation is reversed later in the film when Ali and his co-workers laugh at Emmi, deriding her physical appearance and her age.

The reconciliation scene (obligatory because of the melodramatic model) is set in the bar in which the two first met. As in that opening scene, the two are seen dancing, exchanging the romantic clichés that viewers of melodrama are accustomed to. At the point when all problems seem resolved, Ali suddenly collapses, negating our expectations. In the final scene we see Ali in a hospital bed. He is suffering from a common ailment of immigrant workers, a perforated ulcer resulting from the tensions of living and working in an alien and hostile culture. The doctor informs Emmi that Ali's ailment will undoubtedly recur and soon destroy him, and the film ends with an image of Emmi, sitting on the bed in which Ali is sleeping, staring out an empty window.

What makes this simple, even naive, story a moving and even disconcerting experience is precisely that it opens space for narrativity by thwarting our normal genre and plot expectations and focusing on the social and moral dimensions of the story. This occurs on an obvious level in Fassbinder's modification of the conventional Hollywood love story: the age difference between the two, their racial and cultural differences, their working-class backgrounds. These modifications, along with the use of other Brechtian and non-Brechtian estrangement techniques, defamiliarize the conventional elements of the story, trigger acts of comprehension in the viewer, and stimulate him to think in a socially critical way about the story and about the world of its composition. This cognitive process, although guided by the narrative, is not, strictly speaking, determined by the text; it can only occur with the active participation of the viewer.

Fassbinder has acknowledged that this is for him a matter of conscious design, explaining that his films are "not so much provocative as designed to activate thought processes" (*S&S*, p. 3). He goes on to distinguish *Ali* from his earlier films: "I thought [earlier] that if you brought people up against their own reality they'd react against it. I don't think that any more. I now think that the primary need is to satisfy the audience and *then* to deal with political content. First you have to make films that are seductive, beautiful, about emotion or whatever..." (*S&S*, p. 3). In *Ali* Fassbinder does this by exploiting the potential of melodrama to provide satisfaction with the story at the same time that he negates the social norms and values that identify that genre in order to generate space for viewer narrativity.

Fassbinder's use of melodrama to produce a socially critical response in the viewer has been analyzed by Judith Mayne, who sees *Ali* as "a confrontation between melodrama and politics."[9] Mayne argues that *Ali* exploits a "radical potential of the melodrama" as it has been defined by Thomas Elsaesser: "The melodrama, at its most accomplished, seems capable of reproducing more directly than other genres the patterns of domination and exploitation existing in a given society, especially the relation between psychology, morality, and class consciousness, by emphasizing so clearly an emotional dynamic whose social correlative is a network of external forces directed oppressingly inward, and with which the characters themselves unwittingly collide to become their agents" (*F&S*, p. 67). Used this way, melodrama is no longer a vehicle for escapism but achieves the opposite effect, producing acts of cognition and comprehension in the viewer. Fassbinder's film achieves this effect not only by exploiting the ability of melodrama to reveal the force of socio-political intrusions in individual lives but by suspending our conditioned genre expectations at critical points.

An example occurs in the scene in which Ali collapses just at the point when the viewer anticipates a happy ending. Instead of providing the expected resolution to the interpersonal conflict between Emmi and Ali, Fassbinder suddenly shifts our attention to the complex socio-political problems of immigrant workers, suggesting not only that such problems cannot be overcome by a positive interpersonal relationship but that such problems will, indeed, destroy the chances for such relationships. In effect, the lack of a clear resolution of Emmi's and Ali's problems—either their personal or their social problems—creates a gap at the content level of the story that interrupts the continuity of the story for the viewer. And the gap is one that only the viewer can fill. This is underscored by the final shot of the film and by the withholding of the expected *Ende*. In that final shot Emmi and Ali, framing the hospital window, confront an uncertain and bleak future. The window gestures to the world outside, where patterns of exploitation and prejudice continue to diminish the possibilities for self-realization and personal happiness. The absence of the conventional *Ende* reinforces the narrative's open-endedness, suggesting the barest possibility of change. Any solutions to the problems revealed by the narrative will have to be supplied by the viewer himself. By evoking familiar patterns and expectations and then negating them, the film leads the viewer not only to reflect on certain social problems but to search for their possible solutions.

Fassbinder locates the cinematic beginnings of such negation and subversion of expectations in films like Hitchcock's *Suspicion* and especially in the films of Douglas Sirk. To a great extent *Ali* is modelled on Sirk's *All That Heaven Allows* and constitutes, as Judith Mayne has observed, a "conscious homage" to Sirk (F&S, p. 67). Sirk's film depicts a romance between a beautiful middle-class widow (played by Jane Wyman) and her handsome gardener (played by Rock Hudson). Their relationship meets various kinds of disapproval and rejection until, after several near tragedies, they are happily united at the end. Mayne sees the melodramatic elements of Sirk's films to be "so overdetermined as to function both within the boundaries of intense narrative configuration and as a social commentary which bursts through the confines of that determination" (F&S, p. 68). This is made evident in Wyman's initial choice of family, friends, and middle-class security over her love for Hudson. Mayne points out how the barrenness of this choice is revealed to the viewer when Wyman's children give her a television set at Christmas time: "in a close-up of the television screen we see the reflection of Wyman's face, isolated, lonely, and doomed, it would seem, to a future of passive contemplation. We as spectators witness Wyman's confrontation with the futility of the life which she has opted for" (F&S, p. 68). This image illustrates how overdetermination produces semantic levels of complexity that can only be formulated by the viewer. Like Fassbinder's use of negations, such overdetermination estranges the spectator from a familiar, conventional world and forces him to question its values and norms within a new context of values. To a degree this shifts the scene of the action to the viewer's consciousness.

Fassbinder's *Ali* consciously extends this kind of overdetermination, making it more obtrusive and forcing an ideological response on the part of the viewer. As Fassbinder describes the process, "What passes on the screen isn't something I can directly identify with from my own life, because it's so pure, so unreal. And yet within me, together with my own reality, it becomes a new reality. The only reality that matters is in the viewer's head" (*S&S*, p. 4). This is an accurate description of how *Ali* affects the viewer; the film's highly distanced use of the conventions of melodrama both involves us and alienates us from the reality lived by the characters. Because we are drawn into the story we are open to the genuine emotional appeal it makes, and because we are again and again alienated by the negations employed by Fassbinder, we can take the necessary critical distance to see the story in the context of the larger social reality outside the boundaries of the film and of our own experience.

Paradoxically, it is the estrangement of the narrative through negations, setting up boundaries between viewer and text, that breaks down the boundaries between the world of the film and the political world outside, so that it becomes almost impossible not to develop the film's perceptions in one's own consciousness and carry them back into the world of one's day-to-day experience. This occurs because Fassbinder's use of negations both frames the action, distancing us from it, and then unframes it by opening the frame outward to include us. We have already observed one instance of this dynamic, occurring when the genre expectation of a happy ending is negated by Ali's collapse and the subsequent scene in the hospital. Fassbinder not only breaks the frame of the melodrama but leaves the narrative as a whole unresolved, unframed, open to the narrativity of the viewer, and opening out into his own activity subsequent to viewing the film.

Additional expressions of this framing/unframing dynamic involve both the subversion of other genre elements and the literal framing techniques used throughout the film. But Fassbinder so skillfully blends the various expressions of this dynamic that it becomes difficult to draw form and content distinctions.[10] In general, the basic theme of the film—the objectification and rejection by others of Emmi and Ali and their consequent suffering—is expressed in the film's formal elements, especially the composition of its visual images and the montage. The highly stylized compositional qualities of the film's images express, through literal framing devices and less literal representations of the objectifying gazes of others, the nature of the activity of one consciousness or group as it negates the value of another consciousness or group.[11] By demonstrating the nature and significance of such framing of others in our attitudes and behavior, the formal elements of the film virtually enact the thematic elements of the narrative. And the framing/unframing dynamic of the film forces the viewer to interact with the narrative, recognizing his own role as the other to those about him.

The powerful effect of the other on personal relations is effectively rendered by the relentless stares to which Ali and Emmi are constantly subjected. Throughout the film we see the couple reduced to objects in the gaze of others. The objectifying nature of the gaze of others is reinforced by numerous shots that frame episodes through windows, doorways, and arches. Emmi and Ali are constantly being seen by others, and in being seen, they are fixed, stereotyped, and reduced. The cumulative effect of the various framed shots is to make the viewer conscious of his own role in objectifying and stereotyping others and thus limiting their possibilities and their potential for happiness.

Fassbinder establishes the perniciousness of the objectifying look in the opening sequences of the film when Emmi and Ali first meet in the pub. Emmi has come in to get out of the rain. As she stands hesitantly in the doorway the Arab patrons at the bar stare at her. She is clearly out of place here, an intruder in an alien environment. Her status as an outsider is further registered through the Arabic music on the jukebox, the overall static impression of the scene, and the minimal use of language that results in almost unendurable silences.[12] The static quality of the scene is produced through a reduction of movement and action. Actors simply stand and stare; there is almost no camera movement. The shot/reverse shot technique (F&S, pp. 73-74) establishes the basic gesture of the scene, the act of looking. It also exemplifies the reciprocal nature of the look: just as Emmi is fixed in the gaze of others, she objectifies others through her gaze. When Ali and Emmi dance, the stares of the other patrons seem to intensify. Now the two of them are reduced to objects in the gaze of others, limited by the collective stare that signifies the rejection of any relationship on their part.

This objectifying, fixating look of others is developed in numerous subsequent episodes as the basic mechanism of the hostility and prejudice that the two experience: neighbors gaze at them through windows and screens; Emmi's fellow workers isolate her behind railings and staircases. This culminates in an intense emotional scene in a large outdoor cafe where Emmi breaks down and weeps because she is unable to endure any longer the rejection and isolation. Through several long shots the viewer sees the couple isolated in a sea of empty tables, brutally ostracized by those about them. As the scene is played out, the camera cuts to the cold, impassive faces of the waiters and staff who are staring from a distance at the two isolated figures.

For the most part, these various framing devices serve to distance the viewer from the action of the narrative, continually reminding us that we are watching an elaborately constructed fiction and inviting us to critically evaluate the actions of the characters. Yet the ubiquitous gesture of looking enacted in scene after scene makes us conscious that we, too, are looking and therefore participating in a symbolic way in the action of the narrative (and in a real way in the social world represented by the narrative). This is most forcibly rendered when Fassbinder breaks the frame, opening it to include us, during a restaurant scene that takes place on Emmi and Ali's wedding day. Here, too, we see a waiter who stares unremittingly, Emmi and Ali, unaccustomed to ordering from so complex a menu, look clumsy and disoriented in this environment. As we observe them in their embarrassment, we become implicated in the gaze that reduces them to objects. Then, all alone on screen, framed by an archway, Emmi and Ali stare directly back at us, the film audience.

By thus extending the shot/reverse shot technique to include the audience, Fassbinder forces the viewer to recognize that this kind of objectification pervades not only the fictional world on the screen but his own social and phenomenal world, and, further, that the social dynamics represented here are an extension of a fundamental reciprocal relationship of one consciousness and another. By symbolically implicating the viewer in the suffering of Emmi and Ali, Fassbinder forces him to come to the conclusion reached by existentialist philosophy: that morality among men consists in restricting one another's freedom as little as possible. The objectification of others, whether as individuals or as whole social groups, seeks to deny their freedom and virtually to destroy their existence as free beings. Thus Emmi's initial experience of objectification and rejection in the opening sequence is emblematic of her and Ali's subsequent suffering, and that suffering can stand as a model of the kind of prejudice and hostility that *Gastarbeiter* in Germany experience continually and on a larger scale.

The responsibility for that suffering, Fassbinder demonstrates, rests with each individual, to the degree that he fails to respect the integrity of each other human freedom. Fassbinder underscores this recognition with other framing devices and negations related to the objectification of Emmi and Ali by one another. Their interpersonal conflict becomes a model, writ small, of the societal cruelty to which they had earlier been subjected. Because they had sought to protect one another from that cruelty, their own lapse into similar behavior increases the stakes, however. We witness Ali's acute anguish at Emmi's objectification of him and Emmi's desolation at Ali's rejection of her, and we feel an intense sympathy for them. But we also feel a measure of contempt for them because of the callousness they demonstrate toward one another. Emmi strikes us as petty when she refuses so small a consideration as preparing an Arab meal for Ali; Ali seems heartless when he stands laughing at Emmi with his fellow mechanics in the garage. Fassbinder skillfully plays our feelings off against one another, drawing us into the story by revealing the pain and desperation of his characters, forcing us to stand back and judge by negating our sense of their worthiness.

By the end of the film we see both Emmi and Ali as victims of society, of one another, and even of ourselves. But Ali is most unequivocally the victim, and at the open end of the narrative we are forced to take our place next to Emmi, sharing her sense of responsibility for his future. In bringing us to this sense of responsibility, *Ali* has gone beyond any mere representational capacity of film since the possibilities for balancing the tensions between self and other depicted here are rooted in the viewer's conscious participation; the tensions are not resolved on the screen. By making familiar codes of melodrama unfamiliar and by leaving tensions unresolved, *Ali* provides space for viewer reflexivity and focuses our critical concern on the social world and its constraints on individual possibilities. Any potential resolution of the problems depicted here must emerge on the other side of what is given in the film and can only be provided by the viewer himself.

Both *The American Friend* and *Ali* replace the voyeuristic qualities of traditional narrative cinema with structures of indeterminacy that involve the viewer actively in the production of meaning. The former dislocates the viewer from a comfortable, canny world into an uncanny world that is truer to the condition of an examined consciousness. In doing so it draws the viewer towards an examination of his own experience as a situated, yet open consciousness. The latter estranges the viewer sufficiently from the narrative and from his own role as viewer to enable him to see the dynamics of his own involvement in the suffering of others on both an individual and a social level. Both films demonstrate not just the role of the reader in producing the meaning of texts but the way in which the exploitation of the reader's role enhances the possibilities of narrative.

*Florida State University*

## NOTES

[1] To bring some order to this diversity Wolfgang Iser makes a useful distinction between *Wirkungstheorie* and *Rezeptionstheorie*. Although both focus on readers, the former is based on phenomenological premises and proposes a "theory of aesthetic response" that studies the process of readers experiencing texts. The latter, using positivistic methods, is more properly designated "reception theory" since it studies the social conditions of a text's production and the history of its consumption. For a discussion of the fundamental differences between these two approaches see Peter Uwe Hohendahl, "Introduction to Reception Aesthetics," *New German Critique*, 10 (Winter 1977), 29-63. For a comparison of the various phenomenologically based reading models (including those of Stanley Fish, David Bleich, Norman Holland, Wolfgang Iser, and Jonathan Culler) see Steven Mailloux, "Reader-Response Criticism?" *Genre*, 10 (1977), 413-31. In the essay at hand I follow Iser's phenomenological and dialectical model as set forth in his *The Act of Reading: A Theory of Aesthetic Response* (Baltimore: Johns Hopkins Univ. Press, 1978), subsequently cited within the text as *AR*, and *The Implied Reader: Patterns of Communication from Bunyan to Beckett* (Baltimore: Johns Hopkins Univ. Press, 1974). The former contains critical summaries of the approaches of Michael Riffaterre, Fish, Erwin Wolff, Holland, and others.

[2] Iser's approach is best identified by his focus on "preexisting structures" in the text which prestructure (but do not entirely determine) reader response. Hence Iser's emphasis on the interaction between text and reader as "a dynamic happening." This acknowledgement of "textual structures" that induce reader activity argues against the objection of arbitrariness that some other reader-response models are open to.

[3] Robert Scholes, "Narration and Narrativity in Film," *Quarterly Review of Film Studies*, 1 (1976), 286, hereafter cited within the text as NN.

[4] George Bluestone, *Novels into Film* (1957; rpt. Berkeley: Univ. of California Press, 1968), pp. 47-48.

[5] Michael Covino, "Wim Wenders: A Worldwide Homesickness," *Film Quarterly*, 31 (Winter 1977-78), 16.

[6] Patricia Highsmith, *Ripley's Game* (New York: Pyramid Books, 1977), p. 5.

[7] *Brecht on Theatre,* trans. John Willet (New York: Hill and Wang, 1964), p. 192. I have changed Willet's translation from "alienates" to the more appropriate "estranges."

[8] "Forms of Address: Tony Rayns Interviews Three German Filmmakers," *Sight and Sound,* 44 (Winter 1974-75), 3, subsequently cited within the text as S&S.

[9] Judith Mayne, "Fassbinder and Spectatorship," *New German Critique,* 12 (Fall 1977), 65, subsequently cited within the text as F&S. I am indebted to Mayne's penetrating essay for a number of insights into the political significance of the melodramatic elements of *Ali* and of the reifying gaze.

[10] Fassbinder achieves a similar marriage of form and content in *Despair,* where the multiplied reflective surfaces of the film's sets constitute expressive analogues for various aspects of the protagonist's psychological condition, the relationships of the film's characters, and the film's complex treatment of the *doppelgänger* theme. These reflective yet transparent surfaces express the alienation of the characters, the superficiality of their relationships, the ambiguity of the psychological self, and the persistence of the individual being reflected back in one's mirrored image.

[11] Jean-Paul Sartre has exhaustively explored the dynamics and philosophical significance of the look or gaze in his monumental phenomenological work *Being and Nothingness,* trans. Hazel E. Barnes (New York: Philosophical Library, 1948).

[12] For an analysis of the functions of language and the significance of long silences in *Ali* see James C. Franklin, "Method and Message: Forms of Communication in Fassbinder's *Angst Essen Seele Auf,*" *Literature/Film Quarterly,* 7 (1979), 182-200.

# Mediation, the Novelistic, and Film Narrative

## JUDITH MAYNE

The title of Edmundo Desnoes' 1967 Cuban novel, *Inconsolable Memories,* designates a fundamental function of narrative. Specifically, the "inconsolable memories" of this novel suggest the connections between the novel and the cinema as narrative forms. The protagonist of the novel, Sergio, is a writer who has remained in Cuba after the revolution, while his family and friends have moved to the United States. The novel is written as Sergio's journal, and his ambiguous relationship to the Cuban revolution emerges as he narrates the events of his life. Sergio is an observer, a spectator. The act of writing for him is both distance from and participation in the world around him. Film viewing provides, in the novel, a metaphor for Sergio's desire to participate from the comfortable vantage point of a spectator's seat: "I went to the movies to get away from flesh-and-blood people. . . . I like to have the images surround me and engulf me."[1] The film which Sergio has gone to see is *Hiroshima mon amour,* from which comes the title of the novel: "She [Emmanuèlle Riva] said something that stuck in my head: 'J' ai désiré avoir une inconsolable memoire.' I suspect civilization is just that: knowing how to relate things, not forgetting anything. That's why civilization is impossible here: Cubans easily forget the past: they live too much in the present."[2] There is a fundamental connection, in *Inconsolable Memories,* between cinema, the journal as novel form, and Sergio's social identity. Sergio is always a spectator—whether as literal spectator in a movie theater, as a writer, or as observer of the world around him. Like the Riva character of *Hiroshima mon amour,* who attempts to solidify memory by binding together in her consciousness as many images of Hiroshima as possible, Sergio relies on the mediating capacities of words and images to create a sense of totality, to establish connections.

The term "mediation" describes this function common to novels and films: as readers and as spectators, we participate in an imaginary world contained within the immediate grasp of the screen and the text, but drawn from the world beyond their limits. While the words and images of narrative may not always be totally constitutive of a social identity, as is the case with Sergio, they are at very least informed by a social attitude, suggesting that narrative mediates between readers/viewers, and the world beyond the boundaries of the text.

In marxist discourse, mediation refers to the variety of institutions and objects which connect socioeconomic reality both to the realms of the superstructure and to individual experience.[3] Put another way, mediations are the areas through which socioeconomic reality is channeled. In *Search for a Method,* Jean-Paul Sartre argues for the serious study of mediations, not as simple vehicles but as complex determinations. Unlike other terms which have been used to describe the relations between individual experience and social reality, such as reflection, the very word "mediation" suggests that the path from social reality to individual experience and expression is full of detours, margins, and complex turns. Sartre reproached the Marxism of his time for its failure to show the genesis of the relation between, for example, Flaubert's realism and its class origins. Always omitted from the marxist account, says Sartre, is the real significance of the phrase: "belonged to the bourgeoisie."[4] Class identity begins with the family, and so Sartre's analysis of Flaubert's life and work begins with the author's family—a "mediation between the universal class and the individual."[5] While bourgeois narrative may not have the same centrality as the nuclear family, it, too, is a mediating institution between the universal class and the individual.

The term "mediation" has also acquired a specific literary meaning. René Girard has described the nature of desire in the novel as mediated: characters do not desire spontaneously, but in imitation or emulation of a model which they have chosen.[6] Hence desire is triangular: if A desires B, it is through the mediation of C. Thus, Emma Bovary's desires are formulated through the romantic fiction she has read; Julien Sorel in *The Red and the Black* imitates the behavior of Napoleon. Girard's analysis is concerned with the dynamics of narrative structure. While mediation for him is the genesis of desire as the fundamental motive of the novel's characters, the term suggests as well the negotiation of opposing terms, the resolution of conflict, which characterizes narrative. Mediation thus describes the sense of balance, of cohesion, of reconciliation engendered within narrative. From Girard, then, we retain the sense of mediation as the structuring principle of narrative, and from Sartre, the sense of mediation as a structuring principle of socioeconomic reality and individual experience. In both Girard's analysis of a process specific to novels, and Sartre's analysis of the marxist conceptualization of individual and social reality, mediation is a mode of reconciliation and negotiation. In this context the novel can certainly be seen as an ideological form: a specific narrative means of articulating and understanding the relationship between human beings and their real conditions of existence that Edward Said has chosen to call "novelistic."[7]

Above and beyond the influence of specific novels on specific films, or the transposition of the devices of the novel to the screen, the novelistic determines, to a large extent and in various ways, our social and aesthetic expectations of the institution of cinema. In Western culture the novelistic is shaped by three interrelating social phenomena: the middle class, leisure, and women. The most fundamental of these is the middle class. On the one hand, early novels reflected middle-class aspirations in their themes and plots: the individualism of *Robinson Crusoe,* the Puritanism of *Clarissa,* the reconciliation of public image and self-knowledge in *Tom Jones.* On the other hand, the growth of the novel was marked by a growing correlation between literary and commodity production; it effected mediation between art and industry. The career of Samuel Richardson is exemplary in this respect. A former printer and an avid letter writer, Richardson was asked by two booksellers to prepare an instruction booklet on letter writing. Richardson used the sample letters as a format for moral instruction. He soon discovered that a story was an appropriate vehicle for moralizing and that the letter format was easily adaptable to this end. *Pamela* was the result.[8] The prototypical status of the novel as, simultaneously, artistic and commodity production, is indicated by the ease with which Richardson moved from technician to creator, and by the itinerary of his literary output from one kind of instruction to another.

A primary social function of the novelistic is thus suggested by the middle-class origins of both the subjects of novels and the conditions of novel production. Even more fundamental, however, are the conditions of reception of the early novel, in particular, of the eighteenth-century English novel. The growth of the novel-reading public in the eighteenth century is usually attributed to the simultaneous increase in literacy and in the mass production of novels themselves. Equally important was a more diffuse cultural fact: leisure time. Leisure is not simply time spent away from work, but rather the organization of that time according to class-defined expectations. Prior to capitalist development, never had time spent away from work been defined in quite the same terms.[9] Eighteenth-century English society was marked by the increasing split between the realms of private and public life, between the world of the home and the world of business and trade. The development of a novel-reading public is connected to that split, for reading novels would become a leisure-time activity pursued, primarily, within the home.

Early novels were read most assiduously by women, bourgeois wives whose very accessibility to leisure time was a mark of social status. Novels filled that leisure time. Lady Mary Wortley Montagu wrote: "I doubt not that at least the greater part of these are trash, lumber, etc. However, they will serve to pass away the idle time...."[10] Lady Montagu's reflection invites further inspection, for the passing away of idle time suggests mere escapism. Surely novels also functioned to give dimensions to idle time. Novels, particularly those concerned with moral instruction, gave meaning and shape to the leisure time of middle-class women, who were often separated from the social world of business and productive labor, and sometimes even separated from labor within the home. What I am suggesting is that the novelistic emerges from the division, in capitalist societies, between the home and the workplace, and its attendant ramifications in the differences between female and male realms of activity. Middle-class women were, in a word, marginal to the official realms of history, production, and work; yet the reading of novels offered a fictional world to be consumed and frequent imaginary participation in the world outside of the home.

Essential to this creation of imaginary mode of participation is the illusion of realism in the novel. Even though the term was not specifically used until the nineteenth century to describe the novel, realism defines the aesthetic scope of the novel throughout its eighteenth-century development. What middle-class women saw as realistic about the novel was and is a complex combination of illusion and identification: illusion, because the novel more than any other literary form is based upon the assumption that language reproduces the world and is at the service of a coherently defined universe; identification, because our comprehension as readers is grounded in a shared perspective at once social and individual. There has been much attention in recent years to the ideological foundations of realism as an artistic form that naturalizes by presenting a specific socially-determined view of the world as unquestionable and universal. A central notion that has emerged from these discussions is intertextuality: "Every text is constructed like a mosaic of quotations, every text is the absorption and transformation of another text."[11] With the notion of intertextuality, the ideological dimensions of realism can be understood as textual strategies whose purpose is the containment of experience within intelligible boundaries. Realism is not a stripping away of textual density to allow a transparent illumination of the real world, but rather an intertwining of the authorities of various texts. These work together on multiple levels to produce the realistic effect.

The classic text to which Barthes refers in *S/Z*[12] is perhaps the most fundamental notion underlying discussions of intertextuality, realism, and the sociality of discourse. The classic text suggests a closed system of representation through which readers become passive consumers, manipulated to accept the fictional world as the equivalent of truth. Classical narrative presumes closed narrative, a structure wherein all threads are eventually tied together. At its most extreme, such a definition suggests that as classic text, the bourgeois novel is a conspiracy, a form of ideological control designed to create false illusions of participation.

The notion of the classical text needs to be understood as a mode of discourse more than as a descriptive model of actual texts. In *S/Z*, Barthes distinguishes between the readerly and the writerly. The readerly is the classic text: "This reader is thereby plunged into a kind of idleness—he is intransitive; he is, in short, *serious:* instead of functioning himself, instead of gaining access to the magic of the signifier, to the pleasure of writing, he is left with no more than the poor freedom either to accept or reject the text: reading is nothing more than a *referendum.*"[13] Central to Barthes' analysis is not just the nature of the texts themselves, but the way in which they are read: thus, the writerly is that discourse which defines the reader as a producer rather than as a consumer.[14]

Mediation is a form of reconciliation and in view of Barthes' theory, this function of narrative could be seen as little more than a function of the classic text, a support for the closed nature of classical discourse. If narrative provides imaginary reconciliations, one can easily imagine women readers of the eighteenth century forgetting their marginal status through the act of reading: again we encounter a vision of narrative as simple refuge. The social status of the novelistic is not, however, so easily ascribed to simplistic affirmations of dominant ideology. More frequently, the reconciliations posited in narrative are fantasies—fantasies in which the terms reconciled are irreconcilable in everyday experience. To use the words that Barthes uses in *S/Z*, the novelistic tends as much towards the writerly as the readerly. This is not to say that narrative mediation does not have a function of social control, for it does. Certainly one impulse of the bourgeois novel is the containment of experience within familiar boundaries. At the same time, however, mediation is a gesture through which the contradictions of bourgeois society are articulated.

The novelistic is not a finished product simply presented within the text, but rather a process created and shaped by the act of reading, by the interaction between reader, texts, and social reality. This last term, social reality, is, we might assume, the reality of socioeconomic base in the marxist model or the reality of capitalist development. But just as the specific nature of the novelistic is best understood in terms not of anonymous readers but of middle-class women readers, and in terms not just of narrative devices but of the textual strategies and devices of realism, so the social reality of the novelistic world has specific, strategic contours. It is not just the individual and society which are central to the bourgeois novel, but the interrelating spheres of private and public life. While there are other cultural forms which have, since the eighteenth century, displayed a fascination and preoccupation with private and public life, the novel, and the cinema after it, have had an exemplary function in this respect.[15] Reading a novel is a very private act, certainly one which corresponds to the new credo of individualism and personal consumption of bourgeois society. At the same time, the credo of individualism depends on phenomena like collectivized labor and mass production. Notice that if individualism is a middle-class ideal, it co-exists—sometimes contradictorily—with other realities of middle-class society. Similarly, privacy is not an isolated phenomenon but is interdependent with public consumption. Reading mediates between this individual and social existence, between these private and public lives by smoothing over potential contradictions, a process that is mirrored by mediation within the novel between private and public selves.

Samuel Richardson's *Clarissa,* for instance, describes the tensions between the most important concerns of private life and socially defined roles and expectations. These tensions occur in the conflicts between aristocratic and bourgeois views of marriage, between economic gain and personal fulfillment, between male aggressiveness and female passivity. *Clarissa* can be seen as a novel that expresses the need for an inner life, a shelter from the social changes threatening to weigh down upon and drastically transform every aspect of daily life. More important, however, *Clarissa* traces the quest for a balance between personal and public selves.

Clarissa pursues the inviolability of her personal values to the end, but in so doing she comes closer to the economic terms against which her personal integrity initially seems to be directed. The novel attempts to draw a circle around the sanctity of love, of personal space, and yet all the while documents the impossibility of such inviolability. Clarissa is drawn into a broadening circle of conflation of personal and social values, for she preserves her personal life by regarding her body as her most prized possession, her virtue as something which cannot be sold, her virginity as something that cannot be given away. Clarissa's struggle for an inner life removed from the economic concerns represented by her family is rooted in a contradiction. For in order to defend her personal values, Clarissa must define herself and her existence as property, as commodity—in the terms, in other words, of the Harlowe family.

Clarissa's search for personal integrity is particularly problematic because it is in direct opposition to the desires of her family. Within the Harlowe family, personal happiness is only allowed as a direct correlation of the economic and social designs of the male members of the household. In Richardson's novel, visions of personal life and visions of family life conflict. Clarissa cannot pursue a personal life within the excessively economic demands of her family and the excessively sexual demands of Lovelace. In *Clarissa*, then, a personal sphere is not simply described; rather, the novel traces the contradictions which arise in the pursuit of an inner life.

Throughout the eighteenth and nineteenth centuries, the family is a central object of concern in the novel because, at this time, this preoccupation with the family is a central aspect of private and public existence. In eighteenth- and nineteenth-century Western societies, the processes of industrialization, and expanding trade and commerce, and the concomitant development of an increasingly large and complex public sphere were accompanied by greater stress on the family, the realm of the personal, as the site of human contact and intimacy. In his study of the evolution of the family and childhood, Philippe Ariès designates the eighteenth century as the period of a decisive shift in family function and composition. Gradually reduced to parents and children, the family no longer included the extended family, nor servants and laborers. A former emphasis on the collective, public existence of the family gave way to more isolated, sheltered living: "In the eighteenth century, the family began to hold society at a distance, to push it back beyond a steadily extending zone of private life."[16] One symptom of such a change was the specialization of rooms within the house (separate rooms for sleeping and eating) which "satisfied a new desire for isolation."[17] It is primarily through the family, in short, that the separation between private and public life was accommodated.

> It is as if the modern family has sought to take the place of the old social relationships (as these gradually defaulted), in order to preserve mankind from an unbearable moral solitude. Starting in the eighteenth century, people began defending themselves against a society whose constant intercourse had hitherto been the source of education, reputation and wealth. Henceforth a fundamental movement ... reinforced private life at the expense of neighborly relationships, friendship, traditional contacts.... Professional and family life have stifled that other activity which once invaded the whole of life: the activity of social relations.[18]

In the history of capitalist development, production for many years took place within the home which existed as both an economic and familial unit. However, as Eli Zaretsky writes, "the overall tendency of capitalist development has been ... to remove labour from the private efforts of individual families or villages and to centralize it in large-scale corporate units."[19] The initial separation between family labor and factory labor is tied, as Zaretsky points out, to a second split, "between our 'personal' lives and our place within the social division of labour."[20] He writes: "Just as capitalist development gave rise to the idea of the family as a separate realm from the economy, so it created a 'separate' sphere of personal life, seemingly divorced from the mode of production."

The processes which I have described—the separation of private and public space, the social phenomenon of readership, the development of narrative as a response to the split between private and public life[21]—did not, of course, take place within a short, easily definable time span. The beginning of the eighteenth century, with the rise of the middle-class novel, the changes in family structure, and the increasing development of capitalist enterprises, marks the starting point of a process which continued throughout the eighteenth and nineteenth centuries and into our own. The nineteenth century offers perhaps the most decisive examples of novelistic mediation, since the novel form had by that time achieved maturity and status as an established literary mode. Two nineteenth-century novels illustrate two different kinds of narrative mediation. First the family may be redefined in a search for the proper balance between private and public selves. In Jane Austen's *Pride and Prejudice,* Elizabeth Bennet's love for Darcy grows in proportion to her realization that the members of her own family pursue the distorted identities of immature passion (Lydia) or crass social climbing (Mrs. Bennet). The union of Darcy and Elizabeth seems to transcend class differences because neither passion nor cold logic, personal desire nor public image are allowed to dominate exclusively. Another kind of novelistic mediation moves in inverse fashion, tracing the ways in which love and personal happiness are invaded and eventually rendered impossible by the weight of economic concerns. Thus the heroine of Balzac's *Eugénie Grandet* knows only a personal life and family relations mediated by the constant presence of the gold hoarded by her father, which functions as a literal object of worship within the Grandet household.

The novelistic, then, involves three fundamental processes of mediation. First there is the mediation between art and industry, resulting in the increased availability of novels to a literate public which would become progressively larger, incorporating not just the middle classes and its marginal members, but the working class as well. Second, there is the mediation between private and public self; the process of readership defines the private act of reading as imaginary participation in the social universe of the novel. The private world of domestic life—which, into the nineteenth century, would be identified as a realm more and more isolated from the world of work and production—is thus symbolically mediated with the social sphere surrounding it. The phenomenon of readership brings private and public space increasingly within reach of each other. The spheres of private and public existence define as well the third and central function of mediation within the text itself, a mediation between private and family self. Mediation as narrative structure here occurs in two fundamental ways: through fantasies of reconciliation where the opposing selves of social and personal life are brought together (as in *Pride and Prejudice*), or through the fantasies of reification, where an impossible struggle to construct a private space against the force of economic values is traced (as in *Eugénie Grandet*). In both cases, private and public spheres are reconciled; in the first example, the economic principles of the public sphere are transcended through the family, and in the second, they are not.

Film narrative has, in a variety of ways, appropriated the functions of mediation that characterize the bourgeois novel. The alliance between art and industry, particularly in the commercial American cinema, has long been recognized. Technical innovation has been dependent on the profit principle; consider the extent to which the technical advancements of sound and color, for instance, were dependent on economic gain in their invention, implementation and utilization. In addition, these developments coincided with the increasingly monopolistic nature of the American film enterprise. Like the novel, cinema depends upon the illusions of realism. Realism in the novel is grounded in the assumption that language transparently shows the world. Realism in the cinema is often considered not a function, but an inherent quality.[22] It is often assumed, in other words, that cinema is inherently realistic and that film images are simply chunks of the world cut out and transposed to the screen.

If the novel filled the gaps of the leisure time of women, the cinema responded to another kind of leisure time. The earliest film audiences were distinctly proletarian, urban for the most part and, in the United States, largely composed of immigrants. This was a group of people who had never before been referred to as an audience. The cinema became precisely a means of giving shape to their limited leisure time. To be sure, there is an enormous difference between those bourgeois wives isolated from the means of production who took to reading novels with unlimited leisure time and the early audiences, who with limited leisure time because of lives spent at demeaning labor, were drawn to the moving pictures. However, some basic and fundamental similarities define the early conditions of readership and spectatorship.

Both novel and film have given the illusion of social participation to groups relegated, for one reason or another, to the margins of meaningful activity. Each group occupies, as well, a particularly delicate position in the split between personal and public life. For women in capitalist society, the public sphere exists primarily as a magnification of the personal; and for those laborers who came to watch movies at the turn of the century, there was little meaning to the term "personal life" since home and leisure time were an endless repetition and carry-over of the factory. Seated in the movie theater, the worker as spectator is given an endless series of fabricated fantasies to be consumed, fantasies that allow for an intense personal identification.

The social function of film narrative can, like that of the novel, be described as a response to the split between private and public existence. I am not suggesting that the separation of private and public spheres that began to dominate Western industrialized countries in the eighteenth century functions in exactly the same way in the twentieth century, as if these were static givens of capitalist society. While the separation of the world into work and family, social and personal spheres, has been a persistent feature of capitalist societies, the contours of those spheres have undergone changes. In Zaretsky's analysis of the change in the concept of personal and social life from the eighteenth through the twentieth centuries, a key term is "proletarianization"—the increasingly widespread process by which peoples' relations to work and the social sphere are defined by the factory system, by mechanization: "proletarianization split off the outer world of alienated labour from an inner world of personal feeling." [23]

In short, the split between private and public life has affected larger and larger numbers of people; it has ceased to be a unique feature of middle-class existence. Zaretsky describes the nineteenth-century bourgeois ideal of the family as "an enclave protected from industrial society." Increasingly, the working class would come to share that ideal: "The proletariat itself came to share the bourgeois ideal of the family as a 'utopian retreat.'"[24] For immigrant workers, cinema was a kind of substitute refuge. The cinema offered participation in a private sphere which was otherwise unavailable. Hence in their early definitions as social forms, the novel and cinema accentuated different moments of the mediation process. The novel gave women readers the illusion of social participation, while the cinema gave workers a sense of the fulfillment of personal fantasies. The private conditions of reading seem to merge with the social world of the novel, while the public conditions of film viewing are balanced by individualized fantasy and contemplation. If readership offers participation from the vantage point of the private sphere, spectatorship is, in its early definition, a reversal of that process, offering an imaginary private sphere from the vantage point of public space. Spectatorship and readership alike are accommodations to the changing relationship of private and public life.

Thus the itinerary from private to public space which characterizes the early conditions of readership is reversed in the early conditions of spectatorship. This movement of reversal is one moment in the development of cinema as novelistic form. Yet the evolution of narrative cinema, seen in broader historical terms, has also been one of continuity with the novelistic tradition. While the first audiences of moving pictures were distinctly proletarian, the development of sophisticated narrative films occurred only when film audiences became more middle class. Even when films were defined primarily as working-class entertainment, exhibitors were eager to attract a middle-class audience in order to gain respectability for the film medium. Film historian Russell Merritt has shown how central the recruitment of women viewers was to the creation of a middle-class audience. In order to attract the "affluent family trade," appeal was made to the "New American Woman and her children": "If few professional men would as yet, by 1908, consider taking their families to the nickelodeon, the woman on a shopping break, or children out from school, provided the ideal life line to the affluent bourgeoisie.... In a trade hungry for respectability, the middle-class woman was respectability incarnate."[25] The phenomenon recalls the strategic importance of women readers in the eighteenth century. And as women viewers began to be more numerous, film producers looked to the literary classics—including authors like Zola, Hugo, Tolstoy—for film sources, in an effort to create a more legitimate art form.[26]

Just as the early conditions of reader identification significantly determined the evolution of the novel, so the early conditions of spectator response determined the narrative evolution of mainstream cinema. Particular to the evolution of narrative cinema is the way in which different aspects of the novelistic—private and public space, women consumers, and novels themselves—have been incorporated into a cinematic framework appealing to a heterogeneous audience. Like the novel, cinema has also been informed by classical discourse. The strategies of realism, the forms of intertextuality, which are central to the functioning of the traditional novel have become central, as well, to the functioning of film narrative. The narrative experience of cinema, however, is no more reducible to classical discourse than is the narrative experience of the novel. This is due in part to the historical origins of spectatorship which, like readership, are rooted in the margins of the middle-class world.

In this context, screen and page, images and words, are corollary rather than comparable elements. It has been sufficiently illustrated that there is no language of images that corresponds to verbal language, hence no minimal unit of cinematic signification that can be isolated.[27] However, in a less direct but nonetheless significant way, film utilizes a *logic* of images which evolves from a similarity between the status of images and the status of language in the traditional novel. Both novel and film rely on a special status of representation. Colin MacCabe has shown, for example, how in the classic realist texts of novel and film "there is a hierarchy amongst the discourses which compose the text and this hierarchy is defined in terms of an empirical notion of truth."[28] The camera shows us events which we are invited to measure against each other in a way similar to the interweaving of levels of discourse in the novel: "In the classical realist novel the narrative prose functions as a metalanguage that can state all the truths in the object language—those words held in inverted commas—and can also explain the relation of this object language to the real."[29] The central point is not a similarity between images and words but between strategies of discourse: as novelistic form, the cinema depends upon an unquestioned relationship between image and the real, as the novel depends upon a similar relationship between language and the real.

Film may, then, tap many of the same intertextual resources as does the traditional discourse of the novel: what is understood to be real on the screen is the function of complex associations of different texts. Particularly important in this context is not just the fact that films may use some of the same references as novels, but that the novelistic itself has become, in film narrative, an important element of narrative construction. One thinks immediately of the adaptation of traditional novels to the screen. The notion of intertextuality suggests, however, that the novel informs film narrative not just as a source adapted to the screen, but as an institutional reference. A novel is not simply transposed to the screen, but rather becomes one of the many texts to which the realist filmmaker, like the realist author, refers.

One such incorporation of the novelistic as text concerns the presence of characters in narrative films who function primarily as spectators within the film. These spectators may or may not be major characters of the film. Their primary function is to establish narrative perspective. As is the case with many of the devices of film narrative, equivalences could be established between the use of the spectator within the film and the forms of narration and point of view which occur in the novel. The intertextual links between novel and cinema are more strongly suggested, however, by the fact that frequently spectators within the film are identified as readers. Reading thus becomes a form of participation incorporated into cinematic narrative.

In George Cukor's 1944 film *Gaslight*, there is a rather comic, elderly woman character who is constantly in the vicinity of the central action of the film, but never directly involved in it. She lives in the same neighborhood where the murder of opera singer Alicia took place, and is thus a kind of bystander to the crime which determines the narrative development of the film. Throughout the film this woman functions as an observer: sometimes as a busybody who tries to glean information from servants, sometimes as a gossip who thoroughly enjoys discussing the past and present affairs of her neighbors. She is first introduced to us in a train compartment she happens to share with Paula (Ingrid Bergman), the central female character of the film. The elderly woman is reading a suspense novel, which she describes for Paula: a man who has murdered six wives and buried them in his basement has just taken a new wife. This novel parodies the film we are watching. The elderly woman has, she tells Paula, only reached page one hundred, and so she is certain that more is still to come. Indeed there is, for the woman becomes a kind of reader of the equally suspenseful plot that thickens in her own neighborhood.

Underlying the incorporation of novelistic resonances into the cinema, there is what is perhaps the most fundamental connection between film and the novel as narrative forms: the relationship between private and public spheres which determines the internal structure of film narrative. The narrative function of private and public space is suggested, in particularly exemplary fashion, by the film *My Sister Eileen* (1942). Two sisters, Ruth and Eileen, leave their home in Columbus, Ohio to look for work in New York City, Ruth as a writer, Eileen as an actress. The Greenwich Village apartment they share—their private space—is constantly invaded by external forces, usually male figures, representing professional, sexual, or proprietal authority. The two sisters make uneasy accommodations by adopting a variety of family roles in relationship to each other: Eileen acts as housewife when her older sister goes out to look for work; Ruth comforts and gently disciplines her younger sister as a mother would a child; and when the sisters are frightened by the street activity that keeps them from sleep, they share a not-quite conjugal bed. The women's world is more gently invaded by another male figure, Ruth's professional mentor, who accepts her first story for publication and conveniently falls in love with her at the same time. The romantic resolution of the film marks a restoration of order, as the union of male and female coincides with the readjustment of private and public space to complementary rather than conflicting spheres.

One could easily describe the conclusion of *My Sister Eileen* in more banal terms: this is the happy ending of Hollywood cinema, the requisite formula of successful male-female romance. *My Sister Eileen* concludes with a fantasy of reconciliation (similar to that of *Pride and Prejudice*) where through the male-female couple, a balance between private and public spheres is restored. If the family is central to the mediation of private and public space in cinema, however, the terms are different than in the nineteenth-century novel. Thinking of certain American films, one sees direct appropriation of the traditional novel's concern with family life: for example, *Meet Me In St. Louis* (1944), *Life with Father* (1947), *Seven Brides for Seven Brothers* (1954). Such films evoke a nostalgia-ridden memory of the patriarchal family as resting on firm ground; they also summon up the novelistic as an unquestionably adequate mediation between personal and social existence. More central in the understanding of cinema's ties to the institution of the family, however, are the ways in which cinematic narrative is saturated with familial overtones. Howard Hawks' *Gentlemen Prefer Blondes* (1953) is not on any overt level a narrative of family life, yet the evolution of the plot is controlled, from behind the scenes as it were, by the patriarchal corporate businessman, Gus' father who finally makes an appearance near the end of the film to bless his son's marriage to Lorelei. The family, in the form of the couple, ties the narrative threads together, and the narrative resolution of the film is at the same time a social resolution.

In American cinema, the family functions more frequently as structure than as institution. Consequently, even though the conclusion of a film may seem to correspond to the fantasy of reconciliation exemplified by Elizabeth's marriage to Darcy in *Pride and Prejudice,* that resolution through the family may be more likely to co-exist with the nightmarish fantasy of reification seen in *Eugénie Grandet.* Consider, for example, *Mildred Pierce,* Michael Curtiz's 1945 film which traces the disorder that reigns when the worlds of home and work overlap too extensively: men become weak, women become powerful, children become spiteful. At the conclusion of the film, Mildred is reunited with her first husband, Burt, and they leave the police station together. It appears that the couple functions, once again, as a means of restoring private and public spheres to a relation of harmony. Mildred has retreated from the public sphere (her business is in shambles) that Burt has re-entered (he has found a job). As we see the couple leave the police station, however, there is a disturbance in this vision of order. In the foreground of the image two cleaning women are on their knees scrubbing the floor. Contained within the same image are two visions of private and public space: the couple, representing the idealized balance of male and female, work and home; and the two women, representing a less idealized balance where women's work is a constant, whether in the home or in the official realm of work. If the conclusion of *Mildred Pierce* provides a fantasy of reconciliation, it also suggests that the boundaries between home and work are very tenuous. The process of mediation in *Mildred Pierce* is highly ambiguous with the final images of the film representing the contradictions of private and public, female and male spheres, as much as the desirability of their reconciliation.[30]

Mediation functions both as a means of reconciling separate spheres and of designating the cracks which separate them. Seen from the perspective of mediation, narrative is neither ideological control nor purely individual fantasy. Rather, the mediating function of narrative represents, simultaneously, the limits and the possibilities of individuals within the spheres of private and public existence. Examination of films and novels leads us, then, to an understanding of both the ideological dimensions of traditional narrative and the social relationships to which traditional narrative responds. The relationships between films and novels, between spectators and readers, between screen and page hinge upon the mediating function that bourgeois narrative art of the last two centuries has fulfilled. That mediating function is somewhat like the way in which the silvered surface of a daguerrotype, when held at a specific angle, reveals a crisp portrait of nineteenth-century life. When shifted slightly, however, the image fades to a negative blur, mirroring the viewer captured in the act of seeing. The mediating nature of narrative is located at once in the gesture that adjusts the picture, in the clear realistic image, and in its reflection of the viewer.

*The Ohio State University*

## NOTES

[1] Edmundo Desnoes, *Inconsolable Memories* (New York: New American Library, 1967), p. 37.

[2] Desnoes, p. 37.

[3] For a useful discussion of mediation as a concept in marxist literary theory, see the collective text, "Literature/Society: Mapping the Field," *Working Papers in Cultural Studies* (Center for Contemporary Cultural Studies, Birmingham, England), No. 4 (1973).

[4] Jean-Paul Sartre, *Search for a Method,* trans. Hazel Barnes (New York: Random House, 1968), p. 58. See also Fredric Jameson's discussion of mediation in Sartre's thought in *Marxism and Form* (Princeton, N.J.: Princeton Univ. Press, 1971), pp. 221-29.

[5] Sartre, p. 62.

[6] René Girard, *Deceit, Desire, and the Novel,* trans. Yvonne Freccero (Baltimore: Johns Hopkins Press, 1965).

[7] Edward Said, *Beginnings* (New York: Basic Books, 1975), p. 82.

[8] George Sherburn, Introd., *Clarissa* (Boston: Houghton Mifflin, 1962), p. v. The development of the English novel as middle-class art form has been thoroughly analyzed by Ian Watt, *The Rise of the Novel* (Berkeley: Univ. of California Press, 1962).

[9] The classic study of this phenomenon is Thorstein Veblen's *The Theory of the Leisure Class* (1899; rpt. New York: Viking Press, 1965). See in particular Ch. 3, "Conspicuous Leisure."

[10] Cited in Watt, p. 44.

[11] Julia Kristeva, *Semiotike: Recherches pour une sèmanalyse* (Paris: Seuil, 1969), p. 146. English translation by the author.

[12] Roland Barthes, *S/Z,* trans. Richard Miller (Paris, 1970; rpt. New York: Hill and Wang, 1974), p. 206.

[13] Barthes, p. 4.

[14] Barthes, p. 4.

[15] Richard Sennet discusses the role of the theater in the relation between private and public spheres from the eighteenth century to the present in *The Fall of Public Man* (New York: Random House, 1978).

[16] Philippe Ariès, *Centuries of Childhood: A Social History of Family Life,* trans. Robert Baldick (New York: Random House, 1962), p. 398.

[17] Ariès, p. 399.

[18] Ariès, pp. 406-07.

[19] Eli Zaretsky, *Capitalism, the Family and Personal Life* (New York: Harper and Row, 1976), p. 29.

[20] Zaretsky, pp. 29-30.

[21] Even though I have described readership in terms of women readers, it should not be assumed that male readers are completely irrevelant to this discussion; if the split between private and public life is experienced more intensely by women, that split still affects the lives of everyone in capitalist societies.

[22] See, for example, André Bazin, "The Ontology of the Photographic Image," *What Is Cinema?* ed. and trans. Hugh Gray (Berkeley: Univ. of California Press, 1967), pp. 9-16.

[23] Zaretsky, p. 30.

[24] Zaretsky, p. 61.

[25] Russell Merritt, "Nickelodeon Theaters 1905-1914: Building an Audience for the Movies," *The American Film Industry,* ed. Tino Balio (Madison: Univ. of Wisconsin Press, 1976), p. 73.

[26] Merritt, p. 74.

[27] Christian Metz, "The Cinema: Language or Language System?" *Film Language: A Semiotics of Cinema,* trans. Michael Taylor (New York: Oxford Univ. Press, 1974), pp. 31-91.

[28] Colin MacCabe, "Realism and the Cinema: Notes on Some Brechtian Theses," *Screen,* 15 (Summer 1974), 8.

[29] MacCabe, p. 8.

[30] Joyce Nelson, "*Mildred Pierce* Reconsidered," *Film Reader,* II (1977), 65-70. Nelson describes the conclusion of the film as follows: "we are asked to read the final image in *Mildred Pierce* as a positive resolution.... Everything and everyone have been put back into their proper places: the murder solved, the murderer found, the couple re-enshrined in their correct roles, and women back on their knees, keeping the facade clean" (p. 70). See also Pam Cook, "Duplicity in *Mildred Pierce,*" *Women in Film Noir,* ed. E. Ann Kaplan (London: British Film Institute, 1978), pp. 68-82. Here is how Cook describes the conclusion of the film: "As Mildred and Burt walk off into the light of the new dawn from which all shadow and duplicity has been erased, they turn their backs on another couple, two women in the classic position of oppression, on their knees: an image of sacrifice which closes the film with a reminder of what women must give up for the sake of the patriarchal order" (p. 81).

# Tradition and the Individual Talent: Poetry in the Genre Film

### BARRY KEITH GRANT

Is there a poetic cinema? This is a rather complex aesthetic question, as the diversity of critical opinion reveals. Films can incorporate on their soundtracks discourse imitative of poetry: the narrator's attempt to reproduce Whitman's rhythms in Pare Lorentz's *The River,* for example. Films can also make use of true poetic recitation: W. H. Auden in Basil Wright's *Night Mail.* However, a poetic soundtrack does not necessarily constitute a poetic use of the film medium as such. The challenge is to define the nature of *visual,* cinematographic poetry, not a simple task given the difficulty with which poetry itself is defined. Donald A. Stauffer has written that "Few people have ever been brave enough to define poetry.... Like life, poetry exists in so many forms and on so many levels that it triumphantly defies description."[1] The present essay, therefore, does not seek to establish a definitive definition of poetry or the poetic; however, it does seem essential that a discussion of film poetry be grounded in some sense of, a working definition of, the poetic. Following Stauffer, then, let me suggest that "poetry is not only a way of looking at the world, but a way of speaking about it,"[2] a way that Ezra Pound quite simply yet rightly describes as "the most concentrated form of verbal expression."[3] What follows is an overview of some of the work already done on the subject and an exploration of a logical yet largely unmapped area, film genre. Precisely the unique compression of the visual discourse of genre films gives rise to poetic quality.

The common view of poetic cinema is of a broadly conceived category of lyric as opposed to narrative film;[4] yet this is a superficial distinction which, as will be shown, breaks down upon closer inspection. Maya Deren's notion of "horizontal" (narrative progression) as opposed to "vertical" filmmaking (lyrical contemplation) is vividly defined, but results ultimately in the same unprofitable distinction. According to Deren, the images in a film taking the vertical approach to experience "are related because they are held together by either an emotion or a meaning that they have in common, rather than by logical action."[5] In other words, a film constructed vertically builds upon the filmmaker's perception of an event rather than evolving into other causally-related events. This idea is clear enough when applied to Deren's own work: in *Meshes of the Afternoon,* for instance, she explores through lyrical repetition and variation the psychological implications for the protagonist (played by Deren herself) of only two or three events. In Robbe-Grillet's *Trans-Europ Express* as in *Meshes of the Afternoon,* a few events are repeated and varied, but Robbe-Grillet's exploration is intellectual, concerned with the nature of film narrative itself, and is hardly poetic; in Fellini's *Juliet of the Spirits,* objective and subjective reality in the narrative are virtually indistinguishable. Hence, Deren's direction categories seem entirely inappropriate.

More helpful perhaps is P. Adams Sitney's notion of the lyrical film as a specific cinematic form identified by a first-person use of the camera that, whether it uses a character as a surrogate or not, "reverberates with the idea of a man looking."[6] A particular instance of such a lyrical film might be either narrative or lyrical in the more conventional sense—for example, Brakhage's *Flesh of Morning* and *The Text of Light,* respectively. In the first instance, perception is cast in story form as Brakhage finds himself waking to an acuteness of vision; in the second, perception is presented as a series of abstract images. If literature can accommodate both types of poetry, lyric and narrative, then film, if it is to attain the level of poetic discourse at all, theoretically should be able to do the same. Sitney's notion of lyric film allows for the narrative possibility, yet seems to limit the style and theme of films so defined. Sergei Eisenstein seems to have explored this area in the greatest detail, particularly in his discussions of such works as *Paradise Lost* and Pushkin's *Eugene Onegin.*[7] Vladimir Nilsen has offered an elaborate cinematic treatment of Pushkin's *The Brazen Horseman*[8] which he acknowledges was inspired by Eisenstein. In all these cases, however, the poetry is treated essentially as narrative; the poetic element, whatever it may be, is almost wholly ignored.

The clearest connection between poetry and film may be found in the basic similarity between metaphor, the essential stylistic trope of the former, and montage, the fundamental structural technique of the latter. Hence aestheticians of the cinema—V. I. Pudovkin, George Bluestone, John Howard Lawson, and Herbert Read, for example[9]—have seized upon this relation as the theoretical foundation for a poetic cinema. Again, Eisenstein, because of his single-minded insistence that montage is the basic unit of film language, has developed this idea in the greatest detail. For him, montage is "the juxtaposition of two separate shots" which "by splicing them together resembles not so much a simple sum of one shot plus another shot—as it does a *creation.* . . . in every such juxtaposition *the result is qualitatively distinguishable from each component viewed separately.*"[10] In Eisenstein's *October,* for example, the famous shot of Kerensky followed by the shot of a preening peacock (not present in the same space as Kerensky) presents the viewer with a metaphorical attitude toward the leader of the Provisional Government—he is (like) a peacock, vain and pompous—information contained in neither of the shots viewed independently. In its basic reliance on the juxtaposition of visual images Eisenstein found montage to duplicate the workings of metaphor.[11] Thus non-narrative films that rely heavily on montage, such as those of Man Ray or James Broughton, are generally presumed to constitute the essence of poetic film.

The basic fallacy of Eisenstein's premise, the word-shot analogy embraced so dogmatically by most early Soviet filmmakers, has been argued by Christian Metz. For him, shots are less like words than statements in that, for example, they are infinite in number and are the invention of the speaker, that is, the filmmaker.[12] Metz's argument affects the question of cinematic metaphor hardly at all, for the metaphorical use of montage is limited neither to objects nor to particular shots, but may arise on the level of action or sequence. Both possibilities occur, for example, in *Broken Blossoms*, when Griffith crosscuts between Battling Burrows in the boxing ring and Chen Huan's sexual advance upon Lucy: Chen Huan's struggle with his desire is a physical battle as tough as prizefighting, the pressure of social propriety as palpable as the cheering crowd at the match. Cinematic metaphor may also be achieved through a montage of image and non-synchronous sound, as in Godard's *Deux ou Trois Choses Que Je Sais d'Elle,* where a lengthy close-up of a cup of coffee combined with a monologue of metaphysical questioning transforms the swirling beverage into a metaphor of the universe.

More serious, though, are the implications of Metz's elaborate argument. Since it has no basic unit equivalent to the word, the cinema has no grammar, only rhetorical figures which have been conventionalized through usage. For instance, there is no reason why a fade necessarily signifies a lapse of time; the technique is most often read this way because it is most often used in this way. Thus, the main problem in considering film as poetry is that while poetry, whatever else it may be, is a particular manner of using language, film apparently possesses no language at all. In addition, words are abstract (symbolic), images concrete (iconic); that is, words refer to concepts, while images are tracings of concrete things. Nicola Chiramonte insists, therefore, that "nothing can change the essential and necessary fact that the cinematographic image is an imprint. . . . It cannot become a kind of word; it cannot *signify more than itself*"; hence, "poetry and cinematographic images are at opposite poles."[13] Similarly, Rudolf Arnheim maintains that "Just as a grinning death's-head does not in a film appear as a symbol but as an actual part of the human skeleton, so the connection between two objects shown on a film simultaneously never seems metaphorical but always at once real and ontological."[14]

Here, however, practice belies theory. For metaphor in the cinema is clearly possible without the use of any form of montage. In Chaplin's films, objects are made to seem like other objects within the shot by the physical actions of The Tramp. In Charlie's hands an alarm clock becomes (among other things) a sick patient in *The Pawnshop,* and in *The Gold Rush* dinner rolls on forks become the legs of a melancholy dancer. This metamorphosis of objects beyond their narrow utilitarian function is, for a humanist critic like André Bazin, the basic value of Chaplin's work (bringing him surprisingly close to the neorealist concern with redeeming physical reality).[15] Chaplin's ability to transpose reality at times even operates abstractly: The Tramp, roller skating blindfolded near a pit in a department store, becomes a metaphor of the plight of the worker and consumer in a capitalist economy, the main point of *Modern Times.* Emphasis through close-up achieved not by editing but by camera movement within the shot may, despite Arnheim's claim, raise an object to the level of metaphor: In *La Grande Illusion,* for instance, Renoir dollies up close to the lone geranium to show that it is perceived as a metaphor of his own existence by the outdated aristocrat von

Rauffenstein. On the other hand, it is a critical commonplace that physical objects in film may be seen to function metaphorically by their ubiquitous, even unassuming presence, rather than through a particular technique of visual emphasis. The setting in many westerns or in Hitchcock thrillers often operates in this manner; indeed, what is the expressionist city of *film noir* if not metaphorical?

Some filmmakers interested in the possibility of film poetry have avoided the difficult question of film language by emphasizing instead poetic film's special relation to its audience. In an interview experimental filmmaker Hans Richter, initially resorting to a simple distinction between lyric and narrative art moves beyond this when he remarks that in film poetry the emphasis "has been shifted from asking the audience to understand clearly, to asking the audience to swing with the symbols freely, and to respond to their meaning, whether universal or personal, in an intuitive way, by opening up, by giving itself freely to the special work of art." He adds that this applies to the filmmaker as well as film viewer, for in poetic film, unlike commercial cinema, there is intuitive and spontaneous revision of the script, if it "is a result of the creative process itself."[16] Man Ray, whose films are structured so as to reveal the affinities between material reality and conceptual abstraction, agrees: "One intention of his film ideas he describes as causing the spectator, after viewing a picture, 'to rush out and breathe the pure air of the outside, be a leading actor and solve his own dramatic problems. In that way he would realize a long cherished dream of becoming a poet, an artist himself, instead of being merely a spectator.' "[17] The vociferous defender of the independent film, Jonas Mekas, also considers "that very open, receptive attitude" essential to film poetry.[18]

It seems tempting to conclude that because film has no language as such, film poetry is impossible: the medium can make no poetic demand upon the viewer whatsoever. Chiaromonte believes that because images are concrete, film appeals on an immediate level primarily to the emotions, while poetry "cannot come alive without the reader's elaboration; its power of suggestion is a construction of his mind, calling into play his sensibility, and his intellectual and imaginative faculties."[19] Film images make us feel, not think.[20] It is true that images, unlike words, are first of all concrete, but it does not follow that our responses to them must remain solely on the emotional level. As Read notes, the fundamental aim of good writing is "to convey images by means of words. But to *convey images*. To make the mind see." This is no less important for good filmmaking than it is for good writing.[21] It is arguable, for example, that the images in Frederick Wiseman's documentaries make his films metaphorical and profoundly poetic: to discover in *Meat* a sustained conceit for American society's conformist processing of the individual in the process of meat packing and at the same time to refrain from explicating it for the viewer is surely a visual equivalent to the best written poetry. Moreover, the metaphor fully emerges in *Meat* only when the viewer participates, when s/he thinks about her/his own initially emotional responses to Wiseman's images of the slaughtering process. Fassbinder's early work and Godard's later work are similar, except that here, through the use of specific techniques, the filmmaker encourages the viewer to think on a metaphorical level.

Eisenstein believed that intellectual montage demanded participation on the part of the viewer to establish the relationship(s) between shots. Charles Barr has objected, claiming that this kind of "participation" is merely mechanical, like "the children's puzzle which consists of a series of numbered dots" since "there is only one correct solution."[22] Unfortunately, Barr's point is grounded in the intentional fallacy: while it may be that Eisenstein wished to lead his audience toward a particular conclusion, valid metaphorical connections between shots are not limited to those intended by the director. The Kerensky-peacock sequence in *October* is especially simple and unambiguous; the montage of rising stone lions in *Battleship Potemkin,* however, is capable of yielding a variety of interpretations, despite the expressed intention of the director. For Eisenstein, "In the thunder of the *Potemkin*'s guns, a marble lion leaps up, in protest against the bloodshed on the Odessa steps,"[23] but one may read the images as expressing exactly the opposite. Since the lions rise after the ship's guns destroy the iron gates of the Odessa Theater, they express the power of bourgeois repression and reprisal as seen previously on the steps. To paraphrase D. H. Lawrence's famous remark, trust the images, not the image-maker.[24]

The problem with the view of film poetry arising from audience participation, as expressed, is that the open realist style of directors like Renoir and Altman, because of a reliance upon improvisation and spontaneity as well as a presentation of reality as ambiguous, must necessarily be considered poetic, as opposed to the closed expressionist style of such directors as Eisenstein, Hitchcock, or Lang. Yet each of these directors in a different way clearly demands viewer involvement to complete the meaning of his films. Ultimately, this view of poetry, like Barr's preference for realist technique, is a moral judgment about the degree of manipulation acceptable in instigating audience participation. It also underestimates the complex levels of meaning film images may carry. Furthermore, openness as an ideal attitude special to poetry is itself dubious. This is not to suggest, however that "Film is a poetic medium because the viewer views poetically,"[25] an excess to the opposite extreme; while untrained viewers do bring their stock responses and personal associations to movies, images are possessed of specific elements, are composed in particular ways, and so justify only some interpretations.

Thus far, it has been shown that the definitions of film poetry offered appear problematic when applied to specific cases; all fail, moreover, to come to grips with precisely what elements of film might be said to allow for poetry within the medium. Perhaps, therefore, the question might be approached from another, more pragmatic direction: examining the work of filmmakers referred to as poets might prove more valuable than positing a hypothetical category of film poetry. Since it seems essential that narrative film be included in such a discussion (for, as mentioned earlier, literary poetry may be narrative), what follows concentrates on two directors of narrative films: D. W. Griffith and John Ford.

In his famous remarks on Griffith, James Agee enumerates what he concedes are the director's faults and limitations: an ordinary intellect, an emotional excessiveness, an attraction for violence, even a basic lack of understanding about people.[26] For Agee, nevertheless, Griffith "was a great primitive poet, a man capable, as only great and primitive artists can be, of intuitively perceiving and perfecting the tremendous magical images that underlie the memory and imagination of entire peoples."[27] He mentions some of Griffith's images—the homecoming of the defeated hero in *Birth of a Nation,* the climactic chase in *Way Down East,* Danton's ride in *Orphans of the Storm*—which he sees as being shaped by Griffith's instinctive ability to translate into visual terms feelings that reside in the collective unconscious. What Agee means, although he does not elaborate on the idea, is that Griffith has managed to elevate the shot in *Birth of a Nation,* for example, above and beyond the arrival home of this particular soldier, to represent the general feeling of homecoming.

Griffith was limited not only as noted by Agee, but also by apparent ignorance of how his own psychological tensions were working in his films, most importantly, his sexual desire, which remained at odds with the code of southern chivalry that had informed his upbringing. Without attempting a detailed psychoanalytic investigation of Griffith's work, it is easily seen that the men in his films are depicted primarily in terms of two basic, opposite approaches to women: the libidinous blacks in *Birth of a Nation* exist in opposition to the white Klan, defenders of southern feminine virtue; the physical Battling Burrows is the dark side of the spiritual Chen Huan in *Broken Blossoms;* the swarthy Indians in *The Battle of Elderbush Gulch* threaten rape until defeated by the cowboys of the superego; the civilized Weak-Hands conquers the sexual threat of Brute Force in *Man's Genesis.* This aspect of the primitive poet is particularly apparent in his famous last-minute rescues, when an aggressive male seeks to penetrate the locked doors of a cowering female, clearly a metaphoric indulgence in the prospect of rape, the inevitable rescue a self-punishment for the wish. *Broken Blossoms* seems particularly explicit in this regard: Battling Burrows brandishes his phallic bullwhip as he kicks in Lucy's closet door; the soul (repression) in the form of Chen Huan defeats desire but destroys itself in the process. Griffith's heroines (Lillian Gish's Lucy in *Broken Blossoms* is a good example), shaped in part by the conventions of Victorian melodrama, seem caught in a distinctive sexual limbo between prepubescence and adolescence to keep them safe from his own desire. In her autobiography Lillian Gish remarks on how Griffith became a father figure to his company; "I think," she writes, "he was in love with all his girls—or with the images of his heroines on the screen; I don't know which." She reports Griffith's remark that one of her characters "must be the essence of all girlhood, not just one girl."[28]

Griffith's dimly understood self becomes projected in his films as the dark Other, an operation Freud sees as symptomatic of repression. Roland Barthes further discusses this as strategy essential to cultural myth, stemming from bourgeois society's refusal to admit its own desire.[29] According to Agee, the poetic in Griffith's films is articulated in the creation of compelling visual images especially relevant to American culture; compare, for example, Griffith's depiction of the Indian as a sexual being with the Indians in the work of American novelists Charles Brockden Brown and James Fenimore Cooper.[30] Griffith attained the status of film poet for Agee because he lacked both personal and social awareness (how else are we to believe that he was genuinely shocked to discover that *Birth of a Nation* was considered racist?) and compensated for it by working intuitively.

At this point it will be helpful to develop the proposition suggested at the outset: film poetry exists clearly and consistently in genre films. This argument is based on two qualities which are central to the nature of film genre. First, because of their sense of tradition, genre films rely heavily on visual iconography to communicate meaning: images often are of objects that, as a result of repeated use in previous similar films, have accrued great symbolic value beyond the particular work. In the western a railroad represents encroaching civilization; a mine, industrialization; the calvary, institutionalized law. In the gangster film, fancy clothes signify power and status; the gangster himself is irresponsible desire. The list of examples is potentially vast, and in genre films such images "carry intrinsic charges of meaning independently of whatever is brought to them by particular directors."[31] In the generic context it is clearly possible for an image to function symbolically apart from its ontological status.

Of course a particular director's interpretation of, say, civilization's encroachment upon the West is determined by his manner of presenting, or inflecting, the genre's iconographic elements, but these images are symbolic a priori because of the strong sense of tradition in genre films. Film poetry, insisted Jean Cocteau, must first of all be real, that is, consist of images of material things: "With the cinema ... poetry is made to live a direct life."[32] Cocteau's notion seems fulfilled by the iconographic density of film genre. Aristotle's notion of poetic discourse as a mixture of clear, ordinary diction and "non-prosaic," unfamiliar terms[33] is applicable to genre films: the plots, characters, conventions, and iconography of these movies provide the framework of ordinary discourse, while an auteur's unique presentation of them constitutes the non-prosaic element. One of the great pleasures of watching genre films, after all, is the recognition of the surprising variations a particular western, musical, or gangster film works on the formulaic pattern.

Secondly, genre films may be seen as poetic because of the fact that their generic framework necessarily engages the participation of the audience. The medium of film by its very nature demands audience engagement, for the very perception of a motion picture begins with the synthesis by the spectator of the individual still frames; moreover, the viewer's willing suspension of disbelief is particularly strong in the cinema, where it is encouraged by images and sounds larger and louder than life. However, engagement is possible without participation. It may remain merely at the level of passive involvement; film genre, though, consistently exploits audience involvement more than any other kind of cinematic experience. Because generic traditions, arising out of the commercial nature of Hollywood filmmaking, are comprised of narrative and visual conventions (plot and iconography), a tacit contract between producer and consumer, artist and audience, is established and high audience expectations are created. These expectations are then satisfied or thwarted according to the design of the individual film.[34]

Recent structural analyses have shown that film genres operate on the level of myth.[35] According to Bronislav Malinowski, myth "expresses, enhances and codifies belief."[36] Genre films perform this function by restating, hence ritualizing, our social beliefs, our sense of national identity. For example, the western, in its conflict between hero and town, is concerned not only with the universal problem of resolving the tension between individual desire and social responsiblity, but speaks directly to the importance placed upon individualism and action in American society. It can be shown that, each with its own set of generic elements, the genres of the musical, science fiction, and horror and war films all attempt to mediate, to resolve, this same conflict. Claude Lévi-Strauss has observed that myth proceeds in this task by expressing unobservable realities as sets of binary oppositions between observable phenomena.[37] In genre film, social and psychological concepts are embodied in the concretes of iconography and conventions—as sets of such binary oppositions which are apparently reconciled in the narrative. In *Horizons West,* Jim Kitses lays the groundwork for a structural study of the western by presenting a grid of opposing values which inform the genre; and Will Wright, in *Sixguns and Society,* carries this further by exploring in detail how western films resolve these oppositions in their narrative paradigms and how these paradigms reflect contemporary social and economic conditions.[38] While the scope of the present essay does not permit a summary of these analyses, the point is that in terms of both plot (narrative) and image (iconography) genre films operate on a level akin to the tribal order Agee perceived in Griffith. The generic framework not only allows filmmakers to function as the culture's unacknowledged legislators, but the extent of the genre's codification suggests the proximity of cinema to the condition of language.

John Ford, too, is considered a film poet, and is praised as such by Peter Bogdanovich, John Baxter, and Lindsay Anderson.[39] Ford is associated most often with westerns, the genre of which he was particularly fond and which he helped so much to establish. The western, significantly, is probably the most conventionalized of film genres. Ford, like Griffith, captures a social essence in his images; as Andrew Sarris describes it, Ford's style is characterized by a "double image, ... expressing as economically as possible the personal and social aspects of his characters. And it is this economy of expression that makes Ford one of the foremost poets of the screen."[40] The source of what Sarris calls Ford's economy of expression may be identified more exactly: it results from his ability to maximize the iconographic and conventional elements of his discourse. As Agee did with Griffith, one could list some of the many memorable shots and sequences in Ford's work: Wyatt Earp's walk with Clementine down the main street of Tombstone in *My Darling Clementine;* the sudden appearance of the Ringo Kid in *Stagecoach;* the stage's rescue by the calvary in the same film; the showdown in *The Man Who Shot Liberty Valance.* Moreover, Ford was a master at saturating such images with iconographic meaning. In *My Darling Clementine,* for example, Ford views the character of Wyatt Earp as a proud individualist who accepts the coming of civilization. This is depicted in a precise use of the genre's icons: Earp first goes to the barber who, shearing the visible sign of his uncivilized existence, epitomizes Earp's socialization; the artificial scent of honeysuckle perfume that the barber uses on Earp is commented upon more than once. Earp then exits to the street, links arms with Clementine, and walks toward the church; when the male hero, the individual, joins with the woman, the western icon of social responsibility, the frame is neatly balanced by the desert behind Earp on one side and the hotel behind Clementine on the other. The alternatives represented by town and desert are reconciled in the linked arms of the two characters. This, for Ford, is the base of civilization and its establishment on the frontier; the church at the other end of the street has only its foundation built, but an American flag billows in the wind. Earp and Clementine join in the dance on the church floor, a celebratory image of civilization's incipient victory over the wilderness of unregenerate individualism (the self-interest of the Clantons).

Ford sings the generic praises of the American western myth, his later, cynical westerns, *Cheyenne Autumn* and *The Man Who Shot Liberty Valance*, notwithstanding. Sam Peckinpah, on the other hand, has not been reluctant to criticize contemporary American society for what he sees as a betrayal of that pioneering spirit. The barbershop scene in his radical western, *Pat Garrett and Billy the Kid*, uses the same iconography Ford used in *My Darling Clementine* but in an opposite manner: whereas Earp's visit is for Ford a solemn ablution, Garrett visually appears as a ludicrous dandy. Peckinpah sees him as having sold out to the corrupt and effete establishment of eastern big business. Interestingly, Peckinpah earlier in the same film also makes use of a platform and the American flag; however, the flag is not optimistically placed by a church foundation, but by a makeshift gallows in readiness for Billy's hanging and the elimination of the virtuous individualism he represents in the film. In one chilling shot, children are seen playing by the gallows, one boy using the noose as a swing in the foreground, as the flag flies behind him, a grim statement through iconographic inflection of how subsequent generations have made use of our national heritage.[41]

While Griffith suffered rapid decline in popularity in the twenties, Ford maintained his popularity throughout his career, from the silents to the sixties, possibly because Ford placed his vision within a solid generic framework while Griffith did not. Griffith sought justification in history (*Birth of a Nation*, said Woodrow Wilson, was "like writing history with lightning"); Ford moved in the realm of myth ("When the legend becomes fact, print the legend," says the newspaper editor in *Liberty Valance*). History is continually rewritten by cultural myths, and genre films are shaped by these myths; indeed, they help write them. In the popular cinema, perhaps it is the makers of genre films who most demonstrably possess that historical sense, "a perception, not only of the pastness of the past, but of its presence," which T. S. Eliot has claimed is a necessary quality of the true poet.[42] The death of Luke Skywalker's family in *Star Wars* was lifted directly from Ford's western, *The Searchers*, because Lucas understood the power of the mythic element Ford tapped in his sequence: aggressive action in a liberal society is justified when the values of the family are threatened, whether it is set in the Wild West or in a remote galaxy. To paraphrase one of Pound's defnitions of literature, genre films are "News that STAYS news"[43] despite the specificity of their material surfaces (frontier, prohibition Chicago, the sands of Iwo Jima). They are positively bardic in nature, functioning as social ritual, allowing the culture to communicate with its collective self.[44] Genre movies, the staple of commercial cinema, are laden with the stuff of myth, and both their narratives and images may be seen as nothing less than the equivalent of classical mythopoeic discourse.

*Brock University*

## NOTES

[1] Donald A. Stauffer, *The Nature of Poetry* (New York: Norton, 1962), p. 11.

[2] Stauffer, p. 22.

[3] Ezra Pound, *ABC of Reading* (New York: New Directions, 1960), p. 36.

[4] See, for example, Susan Sontag, "A Note on Novels and Films," *Against Interpretation* (New York: Delta, 1966), p. 244.

[5] Quoted in "Poetry and the Film: A Symposium," *Film Culture Reader*, ed. P. Adams Sitney (New York: Praeger, 1970), p. 178.

[6] Sitney, *Visionary Film*, 2nd ed. (1974; rpt. New York: Oxford Univ. Press, 1979), p. 142.

[7] Sergei Eisenstein, "Word and Image," *The Film Sense*, ed. and trans. Jay Leyda (New York: Harcourt, Brace, 1942, 1947), pp. 1-65. See also Richard Wilbur, "A Poet at the Movies," in *Man and the Movies*, ed. W. R. Robinson (1967; rpt. Baltimore: Penguin, 1974), p. 224 for an additional reference to the essentially cinematic nature of Milton's *Paradise Lost*.

[8] Vladimir Nilsen, *The Cinema as a Graphic Art*, trans. Stephen Garry (New York: Hill and Wang, 1959).

[9] V. I. Pudovkin, *Film Technique and Film Acting*, ed. and trans. Ivor Montagu (London, 1959; rpt. New York: Grove, 1960); George Bluestone, *Novels into Film* (1957; rpt. Berkeley: Univ. of California Press, 1968); John Howard Lawson, *Film: The Creative Process*, 2nd ed. (1964; rpt. New York: Hill and Wang, 1967); and Herbert Read, "The Film Aesthetic" and "The Poet and the Film," in *A Coat of Many Colors* (London: Routledge, 1945), pp. 139-45, 225-31.

[10] Eisenstein, pp. 7-8.

[11] Eisenstein, *Film Form: Essays in Film Theory*, ed. and trans. Jay Leyda (New York: Harcourt, Brace, 1949), p. 246. In my "Whitman and Eisenstein," *Literature/Film Quarterly*, 4 (1976), 264-70, I demonstrate through a reading of Whitman's poetry that a careful application of Eisenstein's specific categories of montage may be rewardingly applied in an analysis of non-narrative poetry.

[12] For a complete discussion, see Christian Metz, *Film Language: A Semiotics of the Cinema*, trans. Michael Taylor (New York: Oxford Univ. Press, 1974), Ch. 2.

[13] Nicola Chiaromonte, "On Image and Word," in *The Movies as Medium*, ed. Lewis Jacobs (New York: Farrar, Strauss, 1970), pp. 38, 48.

[14] Rudolf Arnheim, *Film*, trans. L. M. Sieveking and Ian F. D. Morrow (London: Faber & Faber, 1933), p. 265.

[15] "Metamorphosis" is the term used by Gerald Mast in *The Comic Mind* (New York: Bobbs-Merrill, 1973), p. 69. For Bazin's discussion of Chaplin see his *What is Cinema?* ed. and trans. Hugh Gray (Berkeley: Univ. of California Press, 1967), pp. 145-53.

[16] "Hans Richter on the Nature of Film Poetry," *Film Culture*, 3 (1957), 6-7.

[17] Carl I. Belz, "The Film Poetry of Man Ray," *Criticism*, 7 (1965), 119.

[18] Jonas Mekas, "The Other Direction" (1969), rpt. in *Film And/As Literature*, ed. John Harrington (Englewood Cliffs, N.J.: Prentice-Hall, 1977), p. 191.

[19] Chiaromonte, p. 49.

[20] See Jean R. Debrix, "The Movies and Poetry," *Films in Review*, 2 (October 1951), 20-21.

[21] Read, "The Poet and the Film," p. 231.

[22] Charles Barr, "Cinemascope: Before and After," *Film Quarterly*, 16 (Summer 1963), 12.

[23] Eisenstein, *Film Form*, p. 56.

[24] "Never trust the artist. Trust the tale," D. H. Lawrence, in his *Studies in Classic American Literature* (New York: Viking, 1961), p. 2.

[25] Charles Eidsvik, *Cineliteracy: Film Among the Arts* (New York: Random House, 1978), p. 43.

[26] James Agee, *Agee on Film*, I (1958; rpt. Boston: Beacon, 1964), 316-17.

[27] Agee, p. 315.

[28] Lillian Gish, *The Movies, Mr. Griffith and Me* (Englewood Cliffs, N.J.: Prentice-Hall, 1969), pp. 101-02.

[29] Roland Barthes, *Mythologies*, trans. Annette Lavers (Paris, 1957; rpt. New York: Hill and Wang, 1972), pp. 151-52.

[30] See Leslie A. Fiedler, *Love and Death in the American Novel*, rev. ed. (New York: Stein and Day, 1966).

[31] Colin McArthur, *Underworld USA* (New York: Viking, 1972), p. 19.

[32] Jean Cocteau, *Cocteau on the Film*, trans. Vera Traill (1954; rpt. New York: Dover, 1972), p. xii.

[33] *The Poetics of Aristotle*, trans. Preston H. Epps (Chapel Hill: Univ. of North Carolina Press, 1970), pp. 45-48.

[34] For an extended consideration of audience participation in genre films, see my "Prolegomena to a Contextualist Genre Criticism," *Paunch*, Nos. 53-54 (January 1980), pp. 138-47. See also Andrew Tudor, *Theories of Film* (New York: Viking, 1973), p. 139, who reminds us that genre "is what we collectively believe it to be."

[35] See Thomas Schatz, "The Structural Influence: New Directions in Genre Study," *Quarterly Review of Film Studies*, 2, No. 3 (1977), 302-12.

[36] Bronislav Malinowski, *Myth in Primitive Psychology* (New York: Norton, 1926), p. 13.

[37] See Claude Lévi-Strauss, *The Raw and the Cooked: Introduction to a Science of Mythology* (New York: Harper and Row, 1969), and Edmund Leach, *Claude Lévi-Strauss* (New York: Viking, 1970).

[38] Jim Kitses, *Horizons West* (Bloomington: Indiana Univ. Press, 1969); Will Wright, *Sixguns and Society: A Structural Study of the Western* (Berkeley: Univ. of California Press, 1975).

[39] Peter Bogdanovich, *John Ford* (Berkeley: Univ. of California Press, 1968), Ch. 2; John Baxter, *The Cinema of John Ford* (New York: Barnes, 1971), Ch. 1; and Lindsay Anderson, "John Ford," *Cinema*, 6 (Spring 1971), 21-36.

[40] Andrew Sarris, *The John Ford Movie Mystery* (Bloomington: Indiana Univ. Press, 1975), p. 85.

[41] See Edward Buscombe, "The Idea of Genre in the American Cinema," *Screen*, 11 (March-April, 1970), 44-45, for a discussion of Peckinpah's thwarting of generic expectation through the use of unconventional iconography in the beginning of *Ride the High Country*.

[42] T. S. Eliot, "Tradition and the Individual Talent," in *Selected Essays*, new ed. (New York: Harcourt, Brace, 1960), p. 4.

[43] Pound, p. 29.

[44] See John Fiske and John Hartley, "Bardic Television," *Reading Television* (London: Methuen, 1978), Ch. 6, for a full discussion of how the functions of bardic poetry have been adapted to a visual medium.

# Ritual Patterns in Western Film and Fiction

## ROBERT T. SELF

It has been argued that the function of popular genres[1] "is the ritualization of collective ideals, the celebration of temporarily resolved social conflicts, and the concealment of disturbing cultural conflicts behind the guise of entertainnment."[2] The classical message conveyed by change within genre narrative in general and the western in particular is a resolution of the "conflict between the individual and the group, between self-realization and communal conformity, between the anxiety and loneliness engendered by the feeling of the self and the security of passive identification with the crowd ... in favor of the community."[3] Conventional patterns of resolution in the western, however, reveal that the structure of the western formula allows for resolution in either direction, either for or against community. The complexity of values coded into the conflict of civilization (progress, community, culture) versus wilderness (nostalgia, independence, simplicity) is itself reflective of American ambivalence; as James Folsom notes: "The American would find the story of the colonizing of the West of no particular interest were he not himself so unsure of how his life ought to be led, and did he not have real emotional commitments to contradictory points of view.... He wanders tirelessly between the contradictory virtues of civilization and the frontier."[4] The history of the western demonstrates the constant shift—itself ritualistic—in the values associated with this conflict by American society. When the forces of wilderness and civilization are engaged but not resolved, the formula moves from the popular to the aesthetic ceremony where ritual resides not in homogeneity but heterogeneity. It is the purpose of this essay to examine the western formula in fiction and film to discover: the ristualistic aspects of its structure, the relation of that structure to social communication, and the relation in that communication between ambiguity and artistic quality.

Some authorities claim that as the western has developed in the twentieth century there has been an increased tendency for plots to move away from a characteristically pro-society resolution. In the 1940 film *Dodge City*, the Errol Flynn character clearly transcends his initial position as outsider to become the sheriff who brings law and order to the new railhead cattle town, but in *The Professionals* (1970), an ensemble of heroes hire their skills out to, but remain critically aloof from, the moneyed representatives of society. Yet A. B. Guthrie's trilogy *The Big Sky* (1947), *The Way West* (1949), and *These Thousand Hills* (1956) reverses its initial celebration of freedom in the Rocky Mountain wilderness to affirm the cattleman's property, banks, schools, and territorial legislatures; and as a series it posits the option of either resolution. While Boone Caudill in *The Big Sky* affirms the natural order of the wilderness, shattered only by the jealousies of civilization, *The Way West* asserts the claims of manifest destiny as trials on the Oregon Trail that elicit the innate resourcefulness requisite to establish a superior society in the West. Finally, in *These Thousand Hills* that superior society turns out to be the old one from back East.

The effectiveness of any popular genre film or novel depends upon the historically-established conventions of that genre, the audience's conscious or unconscious familiarity with those conventions, and the storyteller's manipulation of both. This is especially true of those individual works which in the process of developing one resolution of the East-West dichotomy imply or invoke the paradigmatic possibility of the other as a foil. William Wyler's film *The Big Country* (1958) employs a series of such structural tensions from beginning to end. The heroic western iconography brought to the film by Gregory Peck (*Duel in the Sun,* 1946; *The Gunfighter,* 1950) stands in opposition to his role as a college-educated, former fraternity man and sea captain from back East who opposes the machismo and western vigilante justice of the Charles Bickford character. The film complicates this conflict further by depicting Bickford's loyal foreman, played by heroic icon Charlton Heston, as negative until he accepts Peck's civilized style. Thus the film establishes a complex anticipation that the resolution will reside with a greenhorn who represents the values of civilization. As it develops, the Peck character is merely taciturn about his skill and bravery (in the best frontier tradition), and although his presence brings a certain stability to the range war that has been raging (through the societal ritual of an engagement), he and the movie finally uphold the frontier values of Bickford and Heston. Thus what initially appear to be confused, contradictory points of view in the film can be read as Wyler's successful manipulation of the double potential for conflict resolutions in the conventional plot in order to effect a sustained level of suspense.

The classic *High Noon* (1952) is significant for its choice of a resolution not anticipated by audiences of the early fifties. When Gary Cooper, one of the most recognized pro-society icons of westerns (*The Virginian,* 1929; *The Plainsman,* 1936) and other films, throws his badge into the street as a sign of his contempt for the people of Hadleyville, he reverses the more conventional coding of the relationship between the hero and society such that "the same opposition of images that represent 'good' and 'bad'—hero and society—can now also represent 'inside' and 'outside' society as well as 'wilderness' and 'civilization'.... The movement of the classical hero from outside of society to inside is transformed to a movement from inside to outside."[5] Interestingly, the juxtaposition of the film with its source, "The Tin Star" (1947) by John M. Cunningham, also demonstrates the double resolution possible to the western storyteller: contrary to Cooper's disgust with the community at the end of the film (though it is important to notice that he rides out of town with his new bride on a buckboard), Cunningham's sheriff (widowed and alone) demonstrates a pro-society altruism; he sacrifices his life for his deputy, to whom he had said about the distance between himself and the townspeople: "I like it free.... You don't get a thing for it. You've got to risk everything. And you're free inside."[6] He establishes his sense of freedom and selfhood ultimately by giving his life for community. In this case the structural paradigm is resolved in the direction of society by the short story but in the direction of individualism by the film.

Stephen Crane's famous short story "The Bride Comes to Yellow Sky" (1898) offers an earlier illustration of the ambivalent hierarchy of values invoked by the concepts of wilderness and society when he makes the historical transition from the one to the other the dramatic focus of his story. The citizens of Yellow Sky cower in the saloon behind the bar leaving Sheriff Potter to face the outlaw Wilson in a manner not unlike Hadleyville's leaving Will Kane alone to face Frank Miller in *High Noon*. The irony of Crane's story is the reversal of expectations about the stereotyped roles of the brave sheriff, fearsome outlaw, and civilizing woman. Potter and Wilson's confrontation has become obsolete and their weapons displaced. The civilizing catalyst of this obsolescence, the bride, is neither editor's daughter nor schoolmarm but a simple woman frightened by her new estate. Crane manipulates the conventional possibilities of these three figures in order to dramatize, if not parody, the East-West, civilization-frontier confrontation as a conflict with no superior resolution.

The structural pattern of conflict resolution not only toward the values of civilization but against them is especially well illustrated by the many narratives recounting the exploits of historical heroes like Wild Bill Hickok, George Armstrong Custer, Wyatt Earp, and Buffalo Bill. William F. Cody provides a rich source of data on the frequently changing values assigned to the acts of western heroes, particularly because his life demonstrates a man enmeshed in a confusion of staged eastern personalities and actual frontier adventures. Between 1872 and 1883 Cody alternated between playing himself on the stage back East and fighting Indians in the West. The confusion of western reality and eastern melodrama in his life is best illustrated by the fact that during the Sioux Wars of 1876, Cody killed Chief Yellow Hand within a month of Custer's death while wearing the fancy stage costume for his role in the play, *Scouts of the Prairie*.

In his memoirs, in his Wild West Show, and in the hundreds of dime novels that bear his name, Buffalo Bill conventionally stood for the heroic defense of law and order, truth and duty, the plots of his adventures inevitably making straight the path of civilization into the wilderness. Yet there have been departures from this pattern. Although Charlton Heston's *Pony Express* (1954) begins in a shoot out with the Indians and ends as Heston inaugurates the official mail link from the frontier to civilization, the real enemies in this film are not the natives of the wilderness but the representatives of another government. The film resolves a conflict between civilization and civilization. William Wyler compounds such society versus society confrontation in his *Buffalo Bill* (1944). Joel McCrea plays the hero as a man who believes "Indians are good people if you leave them alone." He is sickened by the slaughter of the buffalo and the greedy confiscation of Indian land by the advancing railroads. When he takes a stand in Washington against business and government for causing the Indian wars, his reputation is smeared and for a while it appears that Wyler will opt for an anti-civilization determination of his plot. Reduced to working in a New York carnival, Cody learns that eastern children are hungry for tales of the West and so creates the Wild West Show as another reformist weapon in the arsenal of civilization, to reveal the "true pioneer spirit of the West ...: frontiers and freedom, adventure and fair play." Wyler's portrayal of the Indians as victims of evil representatives of society finally asserts a resolution of the frontier civilization in the direction of a society improved by the wilderness.

The hero's conventional role, characterized at the opening of the play by the effigy of Buffalo Bill enclosed in a glass museum case, is significantly reversed by Arthur Kopit in his play, *Indians* (1968). Buffalo Bill, the showman dedicated to help the Indian through his show in the 1944 story, is now depicted as a vain, confused character who aided and abetted the destruction and confiscation of Indian land and who is seduced and trapped by the commercial glorification he experiences in the East. The hero who was moved in the 1944 film by guilt and friendship to fight the greed and destructiveness of government and business has now become an ineffectual showman arraigned with the rest of civilized society for the genocide of the Indian nations. Robert Altman's *Buffalo Bill and the Indians* (1976), a loose adaptation of Kopit's play, reverses the earlier images of the western hero and the image in the play while employing the pattern of dual resolution itself as a subject. Like Crane's story, Altman's film tends not toward a settlement for eastern or western values. It captures the confusion attendant on the historical moment of transition between the two that is frequently celebrated in the western ritual and calls into question the nature of any resolution. The film presupposes the traditional images of the Buffalo Bill hero. The narrative voice of the old soldier echoes the voice that opened each episode of the serial *Battling with Buffalo Bill* (1931). Ned Buntline, the legend maker, describes the literary origins of his hero. Even the unexplained bandage on Annie Oakley's arm recalls the Barbara Stanwyck of *Annie Oakley* (1935), a major part of which evolves around her accidental wounding by her husband (Altman's Annie reverses the favor) and in which Buffalo Bill is the conveyor of truth ("I want the real article or nothing!"). The glitter and pomp affected by Altman's Wild West reflects the musical pageantry of *Annie Get Your Gun* (1950). Within this context Altman develops his wilderness-society conflict in terms of a hero caught between a sense of his personal identity and the demands of his increasingly successful and rigid media personality.

As Buffalo Bill struggles in vain against Sitting Bull to maintain a superior position, the writer, producer, and public relations agent all struggle to possess the hero's image. The real enemy is not the Indian but the eastern taste makers. The forces of civilization win the West once more; Buffalo Bill becomes "America's National Entertainer," and the demands of popular entertainment consume the history of white man and red man together, leaving the Wild West Show where heroes and the wilderness once stood. Altman elevates the necessity of resolution itself in popular genre to the status of enemy, as he captures Henry Nash Smith's understanding of Buffalo Bill: "The *persona* created by the writers of popular fiction was so accurate an expression of the demands of the popular imagination that it proved powerful enough to shape an actual man in its own image."[7]

Built into this structural model, with its double option for resolving the crucial civilization-wilderness conflict in the western genre, is the potential to portray a shifting or diverse set of cultural values. John Cawelti argues that "it is in the changing treatment of this conflict [civilization-wilderness], so basic to American thought and feeling, that the western most clearly reflects the attitudes of its creators and audiences at different periods."[8] Indeed, the pattern of double resolution involves something that might be called the revisionist ritual, a continuing effort on the part of western writers and filmmakers to debunk or demythologize earlier, supposed false images of the hero's actions, to revise and update the hero's image, and in so doing to indicate significant shifts in American beliefs and values. The nineteenth-century dime novel, no less than Kopit's Broadway play, employed the image of the wilderness as a norm against which to measure the failings of contemporary social thought and deed. At the beginning of the movement of American literary realism after the Civil War, the portraits of westerners in Mark Twain's *Roughing It* (1872) humorously debunk the romantic conception of the wilderness; Twain's disgust at the grossly uncivilized "Goshoot" Indians set him "to examining authorities, to see if perchance I had been overestimating the Red Man while viewing him through the mellow moonshine of romanticism."[9] Similarly, "The Bride Comes to Yellow Sky" debunks, under the new influence of Naturalism, both the male world of the frontier and the so-called feminine values of the Genteel Tradition.

The revisionist impulse, frequently motivated by a need to project current patterns of thought onto events of the past, is particularly apparent in the history of the West as it is recollected in the rituals of popular entertainment. Its truth is what we want to remember, the etiology of myth. A recurrent feature of this revisionist ritual in the western is its pretense of truth telling, revealed, for instance, by the depictions of Buffalo Bill. One of the few films of the historic William F. Cody, the joint Essenay-Cody production *The Indian Wars* (1913), went to great lengths to star real Sioux Indians and the real General Miles and to reenact the Battle at Wounded Knee on its original site. *Pony Express* asserted its truthfulness in the litany of the historic facts and figures about the legendary mail service spoken in the beginning by heroes Cody and Hickok, while Altman's film welcomes the audience "to the real events enacted by men and women of the American frontier." Actually, Altman's *Buffalo Bill* participates in the same debunking of the hero characterized by e. e. cummings's famous "buffalo bill's defunct." Cody's image of personal integrity is replaced by a staff of image makers who are professionals of show business. The hero shoots clay pigeons with buckshot, cannot track Indians, wears a wig, and dyes his beard.

This revisionist, what-really-happened impulse and the contemporary attitudes reflected by it can also be seen in the differing versions of George Armstrong Custer and the military. Errol Flynn's Custer in *They Died with Their Boots On* (1941), paints the cavalry hero as a rebellious but successful and popular leader. His death at Little Big Horn helps the army defeat the

Indians and ultimately appears as a personal self-sacrifice required to convince a deceived Congress of the bad faith and unscrupulous double-dealing of the government-supported Western Railroad Land and Trading Company. In 1970, with the United States engaged in the unpopular Vietnam war and historians recounting the genocide of Indians, Arthur Penn's commercially successful *Little Big Man* revised the heroic, pro-civilization image of Custer to depict him as a vain, egotistical, mentally-unstable leader of Indian massacres. In the same manner, the courageous, law-and-order vitality of Wild Bill Hickok, played by Gary Cooper in *The Plainsman,* is transformed by Penn into a foppish, paranoid poker player who dies not in the arms of a beautiful Calamity Jane but with his head on a dusty boot under a saloon card table. The air of history revealed and phony heroism debunked in Penn's ritual reenacting Custer's battle with the Indians is just as unreal today as is the patriotic sacrifice of Errol Flynn in 1941, but both explain the West in terms relevant to their immediate time. They offer their opposite resolutions of Custer with the same certainty which characterizes Kopit's belief that old-style heroes were "written to justify and ennoble a very unsavory, violent, and horrible process."[10]

Unlike Kopit, the concern of Penn and Altman is not simply the debunking of a myth to fit a contemporary sense of historical truth. Confusion and ambiguity inform their representations of the East-West conflict. Similarly, Thomas Berger's novel *Little Big Man* (1964), even more than the film, revised the hero's role to reflect a heightened awareness of ambiguity and contradiction. The hero declares: "I am a white man and never forgot it, but I was brought up by the Cheyenne Indians from the age of ten .... As usual, my trouble lay in deciding whether I was finally white or Indian."[11] The uncertain resolution of the traditional western conflict in the narratives of Altman, Penn, and Berger suggests a period of unstable values. However, to assert high correlation between shifts in plot resolutions and social change is to succumb to historical oversimplification, for western narratives of any one period of time communicate a similar array of options in the choice of heroic solutions to central conflicts. In such cases, it is possible to discern divergent order and values held viable by a particular society. For example, while *High Noon* can be described as a symbolic attack on the repressions of the McCarthy era, *These Thousand Hills* affirms in its parabola of action the traditional middle-class American values reflective of the Republican complacency of the Eisenhower years; and although the community is presented as the villain in *Johnny Guitar* (1954), it still represents the best force of civilization, the good, in *The Far Country* (1955).

There remains, however, a final question to ask about the classical resolutions in the western formula. It is possible to explain the pattern of options chosen by western storytellers in terms of historical shifts in public policy or community faith, or in terms of divergent values offered to a monolithic audience. Is it also possible to explain them in terms of the levels of audience discovered by such narratives? It would seem so. The most popular stories achieve an unambiguous conclusion to the tension between wilderness and civilization; less popular yet aesthetically successful westerns equivocate not only the resolution but the terms of the conflict as well.

Originality is permissible in popular formulae only so long as it strengthens and extends without transgressing the anticipated conventions. Altman's description of the box-office failure of *Buffalo Bill* illustrates his understanding of the power of popular expectations. He admits how difficult it is "to carry people into areas they don't want to go into" and asserts that "the artist and the multitude are natural enemies."[12] Significantly, as Robert Warshow noted, "The truth is that the westerner comes into the field of serious art only when his moral code, without ceasing to be compelling, is seen also to be imperfect."[13]

The concept of resolution around which this essay has centered is crucial to the structural definition of the popular western, as demonstrated by Cawelti in *The Six-Gun Mystique*. "The most basic definition of the hero in the Western is as the figure who resolves the conflict between pioneers and savages."[14] This emphasis on resolution is equally central to definitions of popular genre generally; and they thus far correspond to Claude Lévi-Strauss's famous description of myth: that it reveals its structure "through the repetition process" and that its purpose is "to provide a logical model capable of overcoming a contradiction." Generic patterns of conflict resolution should consequently profit from discussion in terms of myth and ritual. As Lévi-Strauss observes, in ritual "there is an asymmetry which is postulated in advance between profane and sacred, faithful and officiating, dead and living, initiated and uninitiated, etc., and the 'game' consists in making all the participants pass to the winning side by means of events, the nature and ordering of which is genuinely structural."[15]

The resolution paradigm of the western, however, although it sometimes permits solution of the East-West conflict in behalf of the values of either side, also permits a third possibility which hardly resolves any issue at all. Rather, within the other anticipated norms of the formula (character type, locale, costume) it highlights the residual ambiguity of the civilization-wilderness opposition; it heightens the complexities of the tension; it transforms the hero from icon to eiron. Certainly such forms move in the direction of mimetic art but do they simultaneously depart the realm of formulaic entertainment? Of myth? It is here that Leo Braudy says the "implicit self-consciousness of plot" in popular genre becomes "explicit self-consciousness of form."[16] The irony of Crane's "The Bride Comes to Yellow Sky" and "The Blue Hotel" (1898), for instance, is lost to the reader unaware of the major structural and thematic features of the dime-novel western, which self-consciously becomes Crane's subject.

Altman's *Buffalo Bill* similarly calls attention to form by so complicating and magnifying the oppositions attendant on the historical transition from wilderness to civilization that there is no narrative transition of the plot from a beginning to an end. It is a passive, self-reflexive western rather than an active, resolute one. The hero is swept up in a process of continuing transition in which there is never any resolution of tension between the confusing realities of personal history and the inexorable demands of community as expressed and created by the rituals of mass entertainment. The film exploits previous images of the hero Buffalo Bill conveyed by writers from Ned Buntline to Arthur Kopit and played by actors from William F. Cody to Paul

Newman. It introduces a level of self-consciousness into the personality of the hero that comments on the production of the western formula itself. Cody stands between the constantly growing idea of the West imagined and romanticized by white men and the mysterious, historical West dominated by the Indians, who are constantly dying throughout the film. Sitting Bull must die before his entrance into the immortality of the white man's legends, and if the real Indian chief must perish in the narrative in order for a showman to portray him in the ring, so must the real William F. Cody die to the media hero Buffalo Bill. The conflict involves Altman's acceptance of what historian Don Russell calls "the myth that Cody was 'just another scout' who would never have been heard of had not Ned Buntline written novels about him, and who ... ever after lived in a thick fog of wonder, honestly incapable of discriminating between what happened in his life and what Ned Buntline swore had happened."[17] Altman returns to the images of traditional Buffalo Bill portraits and makes self-conscious the metamorphosis of western reality into eastern myth in the William Cody-Buffalo Bill conflict. He dramatizes in one role the same confrontation which occurs between John Wayne and James Stewart in *The Man Who Shot Liberty Valance* (1962) in such a way that there can be no easy resolution between the man who made the legend and the man whom the legend identifies. John Ford's film asserts: "When the legend has become fact, print the legend." Altman's film delineates the tragic tension in Cody between the fact (West) and legend (East) as the voracious demand for novelty in the popular media constantly changes, distorts, and reverses the meaning of the dichotomy.

Such transformations of conventional role conflicts to the point of formal self-consciousness and non-resolution relate these popular works to those canonized in the academy as American Literature, that great literary tradition of the American mind divided between innocence and experience, individuality and community, novel and romance, and inevitably expressed in East-West distinctions. A notable line of twentieth-century scholars from George Santayana to Richard Chase has pointed to the centrality of ambiguity, contradiction, and paradox rather than resolution, unity, and harmony as characteristics of American narrative art. *The Great Gatsby* (1925) reminds us, says Leo Marx, "that American writers seldom, if ever, have designed satisfactory resolutions for their pastoral fables."[18] Moreover, these works may constitute ritual to a smaller, more intellectual audience of communicants for whom significance resides in tension and question rather than answer and resolution. Although the popular audience may not identify with this community, the elite audience is not always distinct from it; both have acquired, perhaps unconsciously, a familiarity with the historical method and form of popular genre. As Braudy has written, "Genre films and conventional forms are generally deceptive because they are so accessible. If you haven't seen them before, you still have a good chance of having culturally absorbed their aesthetic canon."[19] Even while Altman's westerns, *McCabe and Mrs. Miller* and *Buffalo Bill and the Indians*, then, seem to eschew plot itself in favor of poetry, the popular conventions of the western provide the store of images from which he constructs his verses and stanzas and by which his films communicate with us.

Many of the works described here aspire to the level of artistic invention as opposed to formulaic convention. Guthrie's *The Big Sky,* the most ambiguous book of his trilogy is also the most highly praised. We teach the Crane and Twain stories in surveys of American literature. *High Noon* and *Little Big Man* are adult westerns. They are all, nevertheless, recognizably westerns, and as such create a bridge between formulaic and artistic fiction, and their meaning is incomplete without an understanding of the more popular forms they presuppose and complicate. Besides, the pattern of unresolved tension is as much a part of formulaic conventions as is the pattern of social or anti-social affirmation in the conflict between wilderness and civilization. This contradiction of expected resolutions, or the non-resolution of this conflict between cowboys and Indians, settlers and outlaws, cattlemen and nesters, mountainmen and nature simply addresses the western to a different audience. The pattern of plot conflict and resolution described in this essay involves the elite audience as well as the popular audience in the formulaic conventions of western ritual, and represents a significant point of intersection between popular narratives and more complex views of cultural conflict.

*Northern Illinois University*

## NOTES

[1] The term "genre" is used here not to indicate the broad classes of literature (poetry, fiction, and drama) or the modes of tragedy, comedy, and satire, but to designate the various types of popular narrative like the western, detective stories, science fiction, and romance. In order to discuss western narratives at a wide level of abstraction, no attempt is made to distinguish techniques or effects particular either to written or cinematic narrative.

[2] Thomas Schatz, "The Structural Influence: New Directions in Film Genre Study," *Quarterly Review of Film Studies,* 2, No. 3 (1977), 309, and his *Hollywood Genres* (New York: Random House, 1981). See also Will Wright, *Six Guns and Society: A Structural Study of the Western* (Berkeley: Univ. of California Press, 1975), in which he argues that "the myths of a society, through their structure, communicate a conceptual order to the members of that society ... that a myth orders the everyday experiences of its hearers (or viewers) and communicates this order through a formal structure that is understood like language" (p. 17).

[3] Thomas Sobchack, "Genre Film: A Classical Experience," *Literature/Film Quarterly,* 3 (1975), 201. Change in the western narrative has been variously described as the founding of a city, as the hero's transformation from the shaman in a semi-nomadic society to the priest of a stable agrarian society, as the movement from old West to modern society. Since the West is associated with a youthful innocence, the change is said to represent a coming-of-age of individual and society; a corollary pattern traces the fall from innocence and grace as the American Adam figure encounters the reality of civilization. Leo Marx locates the western pattern in the "myth of America as a new beginning" involving Joseph Campbell's myth of the return: "a separation from the world, a penetration to some source of power, and a life-enhancing return." All three of the major patterns of change described by Wright involve the manner in which the hero comes to represent and defend positive social values. See Frank D. McConnell, *The Spoken Seen* (Baltimore: Johns Hopkins Univ. Press, 1975), pp. 152-55; John Cawelti, *Adventure, Mystery, and Romance: Formula Stories as Art and Popular Culture* (Chicago: Univ. of Chicago Press, 1976), p. 247; James K. Folsom, *The American Western Novel* (New Haven, Conn.: College and Univ. Press, 1966), p. 40; R. W. B. Lewis, *The American Adam* (Chicago: Univ. of Chicago Press, 1955), p. 89; Leo Marx, *The Machine in the Garden* (New York: Oxford Univ. Press, 1964), p. 228; Nicholas J. Karolides, *The Pioneer in the American Novel, 1900-1950* (Norman: Univ. of Oklahoma Press, 1967), p. 11; Wright, pp. 29-123.

[4] Folsom, p. 98. Jim Kitses, *Horizons West* (Bloomington: Indiana Univ. Press, 1969), discusses the complex matrix involved in the civilization-wilderness opposition (p. 11). Leslie Fiedler, *The Return of the Vanishing American* (New York: Stein and Day, 1968), describes the pro-wilderness option: "The ultimate westerner ceases to be white at all and turns back into the Indian . . . —to declare that he has fallen not merely out of Europe, but out of the Europeanized West into an aboriginal and anarchic America" (p. 25).

[5] Wright, p. 84.

[6] John M. Cunningham, "The Tin Star," in *The Western Story*, ed. Philip Durham and Everett L. Jones (1947; rpt. New York: Harcourt, Brace, 1975), pp. 209-10. As recently as 1976 John Tuska, *The Filming of the West* (New York: Doubleday, 1976), p. 542, expresses hostility to the film version of this story: "The spirit of the West that *High Noon* portrayed was outside the mythical promise of the land. It may have been emotionally true in 1952, but not before that."

[7] Henry Nash Smith, *Virgin Land: The American West as Symbol and Myth* (New York: Vintage, 1950), p. 114.

[8] Cawelti, p. 194.

[9] Mark Twain, *Roughing It* (Hartford, Conn.: American Publishing, 1880), p. 149.

[10] Arthur L. Kopit, *Indians* (1969; rpt. New York: Bantam, 1971), p. 23.

[11] Thomas Berger, *Little Big Man* (Greenwich, Conn.: Fawcett, 1964), pp. 25, 251.

[12] " 'The Artist and the Multitude Are Natural Enemies,' An Interview with Director Robert Altman," *Film Heritage*, 12 (Winter 1976-77), 12.

[13] Robert Warshow, *The Immediate Experience* (Garden City, N.Y.: Doubleday, 1954), p. 95.

[14] John Cawelti, *The Six-Gun Mystique* (Bowling Green, Ohio: Bowling Green Univ. Popular Press, 1970), p. 55.

[15] Claude Lévi-Strauss, "The Structural Study of Myth," *Journal of American Folklore*, 68 (1955), 443, and "The Science of the Concrete," in *Ritual, Play, and Performance*, ed. Richard Schechner and Mady Schuman (New York: Seabury, 1976), p. 76. In addition to Schatz, Wright, and Cawelti, *Adventure*, see Michael Wood, *America in the Movies* (New York: Basic Books, 1975) and Albert McLean, *American Vaudeville as Myth* (Lexington: Univ. of Kentucky Press, 1965) for recent studies of myth, ritual, and popular art forms.

[16] Leo Braudy, *The World in a Frame* (1976; rpt. Garden City, N.Y.: Doubleday, 1977), p. 114.

[17] Don Russell, *The Lives and Legends of Buffalo Bill* (Norman: Univ. of Oklahoma Press, 1960), pp. 152-53.

[18] Marx, p. 364.

[19] Braudy, p. 116.

# Story, Pleasure, and Meaning in
## *The Scarlet Empress*

### WILLIAM CADBURY

There is an instructive brace of errors about *The Scarlet Empress* which we can associate with Robin Wood's "coherent but unschematic 'reading' " and with Laura Mulvey's paper on "Visual Pleasure and Narrative Cinema." Wood and Mulvey seem incomparably different, the one a prime spokesman for auteurism and a Leavisite New Criticism, and the other a mainstay of *Screen* and its development of "the second semiology," the Lacanian one. Each gets Sternberg wrong because each ignores the implication of the dynamic sequence of *The Scarlet Empress*, the film's development as a story. Mulvey concentrates on what audiences might be expected to make of their relation to "the imaginary signifier" while Wood concentrates on the web of implications, especially those ironically undercutting the images themselves.[1]

Wood argues that the film's apparent cheerfulness is undercut by the implications of its imagery: the film presents a " 'glorious destiny' that is also a progress into ever-deepening moral darkness" (p. 108). He argues that Sophia/Catherine learns "to survive in the world into which she is plunged" but that—and it is exactly here that I think he is wrong—"her triumph over it is won at the cost of becoming identified with it" (p. 112). The true feeling that Catherine should have been able to express for her natural partner Alexei is blocked, so that "Each of Sophia's natural responses is frustrated and perverted, her energies channeled into increasingly unnatural drives" (p. 104), into "sterile revenge and the exercise of power" (p. 112). The effect of the whole is of an allegory of "the soul, stifled to death within the protective shell of will-power and brutalization" (p. 100), with a quality of "tragic-ironic pessimism" (p. 104) and in a tone of "intensity and anguish" (p. 99).

Wood is quite right to take the film seriously, and to follow the "interrelatedness of its motifs and the significant development of its imagery" (p. 113), the "intricate pattern of echoes and substitutions" (p. 109). To "abandon chronology," however, and treat only the implications of motifs and imagery which give a film like this "the intensity of great poetry" (pp. 109, 113), is to ignore the interaction of this network with other sets of implications. The story, while in one sense the progress of the imagery, is surely also a rendition, in a classic film like this, of a particularized character's experience, a rendition we just cannot ignore. Images qualify, but they cannot replace, the implications of the ways characters are shown responding to issues, devising solutions, developing modes of conduct upon which surely we are encouraged to reflect and from which we rightly generalize as we come to our sense of a work's theme.

Wood's reading is merely incomplete, then, a failure of method. Mulvey likewise ignores the development and implications of story, but it is because of an unacceptable aesthetic, an affective criticism which does not trace relations at all but rather predicts responses in an audience on the basis of psychological theory. Her attention, like Wood's, is on the images, but only insofar as they evoke "visual pleasure," a pleasure which "reflect[s] the psychical obsessions of the society which produced it" (p. 8), and in terms of which alone we should analyze (in order to reject, with only "sentimental regret" [p. 18]), classic films like Sternberg's.

That visual pleasure attends "the look," what we (but I should say "we men," for it is Mulvey's point that there is little here for women) go to the movies to indulge, and a complex form of which is encouraged in Sternberg. There are simple visual pleasures played on by classical cinema: the pleasure of seeing the erotic object and the pleasure of identifying with the hero who looks at and controls the looked-at, the woman. There must also be another pleasure, since "the look, pleasurable in form, can be threatening in content" (p. 11). Because "the female form . . . speaks castration and nothing else" (p. 6), men (to whose patriarchal unconscious movies speak, like everything else in a patriarchal symbolic order) are reminded, by the look, of the possible revelation of that lack which "threatens to evoke the anxiety it originally signified" (p. 13). Two solutions, both involving a defensive pleasure, emerge. As in *film noir* or, with more complexity, in Hitchcock, there is "preoccupation with the reenactment of the original trauma (investigating the woman, demystifying her mystery), counterbalanced by the devaluation, punishment or saving of the guilty object" (p. 13). Narrative sequence, the simple tracking of the hermeneutic, looms large in such pleasure.[2] But there is also an anti-narrative, anti-revelatory "look" to balance "sadistic voyeurism"; namely, a "voyeuristic fetishism" which turns "the represented figure itself into a fetish so that it becomes reassuring rather than dangerous (hence over-valuation, the cult of the female star)" (p. 14). Fetishism looks very hard at—so as not to have to look further—that place beyond which the phallus would be missing. For instance, it looks at nets, veils, gauzes, streamers, furs, feathers, anything that is pubic hair or underwear or both.

Here, of course, with regard both to Dietrich the star and the mise-en-scène in which she appears, we are in Sternberg country. Dietrich is there neither for a sadistic voyeurism nor for a hero with whom we can easily identify but for our own fetishistic look. The star's "visual presence tends to work against the development of the story line, to freeze the flow of action in moments of erotic contemplation" (p. 11)—it is here that we will directly challenge Mulvey—and "Sternberg provides the ultimate fetish, taking it to the point where the powerful look of the male protagonist (characteristic of traditional narrative film) is broken in favour of the image in direct erotic rapport with the spectator" (p. 14).

The connotations of images in our culture are well brought out, if only along a certain axis, by Lacanian psychoanalysis. Study along Lacanian lines can help tease out the meanings of parts on the way to attaining, by what Monroe C. Beardsley calls the principles of "plentitude" and "congruence," a sense of a whole film's meaning.[3] But the problem with the Mulvey line of argument is that it treats connotations not as elements of the film, from which design and qualities can be perceived, but as triggers for direct audience response. This visual pleasure attending the connotation of the woman's image as to-be-looked-at-in-a-fetishistic-way[4] is an as-if-mechanical effect upon a (male) audience. Its aesthetic presumes that description should be of audience response: a film is what its audience takes it to be.

Beardsley rightly points out, concerning psychological definitions of aesthetic value and affective descriptions, that there always remains an open question whether an audience ought to respond as it does, and an open possibility that on mature reflection people might respond differently from the ways they do at first.[5] The open question can only be settled by looking not at the audiences, no matter how adeptly their deepest nature is anatomized, but at the works, to see what it is the audiences ought finally to respond to and what their mature reflection ought to lead them to think. To look at the works is no longer to be affective, but objective, like Wood not Mulvey. We might be tempted to yield to the pleasures of a fetishistic look, yet be uncomfortably aware, as we try to do justice to the whole film, of the dimension in which the looked-at ought to be considered a complex moral agent like ourselves, not a simple object of fantasy. Our visual pleasure of the fetishistic sort ought certainly, then, to intersect subtly with pleasures of quite different sorts: the pleasure of aesthetic experience, for one, that, as Beardsley points out, psychological definitions and affective criticism usually intend to explain away.[6]

F. C. Bartlett, long ago reminded us that "where consciousness comes in" is for an organism to be able "to round upon its own 'schemata' and to construct them afresh," to derive and entertain new organizations, new meanings (much as one can generate an unlimited number of sentences from finite resources when one knows a language).[7] Works can be contemplated and hence they can suggest, through their systems of connotation, reflections on issues which psychological definitions of value treat as determined. Indeed, *The Scarlet Empress* raises just the Mulvey issues, not as stimulus for our response, but as a complex of objects of contemplation and subjects of commentary through the whole film's form. Wood, pleading limitations of space, drops analysis of sequence in *The Scarlet Empress* and skirts the implications of story on the image patterns; Mulvey deals only with typical Sternberg images and their putative effects on audience psyches and avoids the same thing, the relation of those images to the story they help tell. Let us look at the story of Sophia become Catherine, the Scarlet Empress, and see how different a picture from Wood's and Mulvey's is provided by its actual development.

In outline, Catherine's story is a coming to private awareness and then to action, such as we see in Sternberg's stories of Thunderbolt, Bull Weed in *Underworld,* Bill Roberts in *The Docks of New York,* Madeline and Doc in *Shanghai Express,* Amy Jolly in *Morocco,* Agent X-27 in *Dishonored,* Helen Faraday in *The Blonde Venus,* Concha Perez in *The Devil Is a Woman,* Claudius in *I, Claudius,* Anna/Olga in *Jet Pilot* and Keiko in *The Saga of Anatahan.* In each case, promises are withdrawn and one is on one's own, but, with substantial doses of a saving irony in the face of isolation, one can create a privately satisfying world of action and enjoyment by recognizing and rejecting conventional moralisms and idealisms as devices for one's subjugation.[8] The flow of the story of *The Scarlet Empress* begins with the establishment of just such a set of devices, and Princess Sophia begins by dutifully obeying her petty-princeling family, her Polonian father, gaggle of aunts, and pompous mother.

I am not one who thinks Sternberg tried but failed to present Dietrich here as an innocent.[9] Rather she is, as always, one of us (presented more for attitudinal than erotic rapport with the audience) dropped into a world where ironic amusement is both a duty and a pleasure. In effect, Sophia's wide-eyed quality is an image of innocence as Dietrich would and does play it, not the innocence of the Princess Sophia Frederica herself. But this aware Sophia/Dietrich is being promised that the absurdities of the opulent Russian world are for her, will bring her satisfactions for which she is willing to wait, and so it is perfectly credible that she dutifully kiss her aunts' hands, believe Alexei's marvelous tale of the perfect bridegroom, refuse his own embraces and his wonderfully masochistic rumblings, and look about her, on the fairy-tale trip to Russia, with a wide-eyed wonder we are glad to laugh at and to share: the world rushes by in panoply and movement, and all is to come.

The beckoning world, one soon discovers, is not just designed to give Catherine things. The doctor is demeaning even if his own wig does fall off. The Empress is a fishwife. Peter with his whirling soldiers is crazy. Everything is too barbaric and too big, everything necessitates an over-styled dreamlike effort. The whole of the first part of the film, with its constant emphasis on Catherine's existence within and her looking out at a world going its own way and using her as it does so, is summed up in the wedding. It contrasts the extraordinary opulence of the cathedral, presented in long tracking shots as a spectacle over which the Empress presides, to the interior experience of Catherine, presented in progressively closer shots as she comes to an awareness of the distance between her selfhood and the use made of it by this travesty.

The breath on the candle, almost putting it out, indicates both the tremulousness of life and its tenacity. Catherine is seen ever closer as the candle flame is in ever more danger of going out. The breathless intimacy escalates and we are shown unequivocally how the passage is grounded in Catherine's story and takes its force from it. While Peter with mechanical and jerky movements gobbles the eucharist and darts his glances around, Catherine keeps looking up at Alexei. Her eyes first brighten, then glisten, then fill with tears. Finally she gives one long beseeching and, above all, reproachful look and Alexei's eyes and head drop exactly as they will when, at the end, Catherine leaves him in the room at the bottom of the stairs as Orlov comes up to her. Catherine is obedient but imprisoned at the wedding, and Alexei is both aware of how she deserves better and at the same time willing (as he always is) to betray her for the sake of his political accommodation in the court whose values he can never, unlike Catherine, transcend.

Despite our extraordinary rapport with the veiled Dietrich image, the for it, nor when she drops it and accepts the guardsman Lieutenant Dmitri. We are shown the nature of the sexual abandon she is accepting in place of what she had thought was Alexei's true love as she clings to Dmitri's back, drops the locket she has gone to find, digs her fingers in a little, and then lets her hands sag in being carried away.[11] The betrayal by Alexei, who had been an image for her of a true love counter to the perversity all around her, leads her to this choice of sensualism, but the way the locket fell through the trees into the enchanted garden tells us that her choice is the right one. It perfectly expresses the Sternberg attitude that autonomy and wisdom are better than ignorant innocence, and that they are reached through an initial coming to terms with the sensuality and objectivity of the world. Catherine's way will, as the locket shows us, be different from those of the Empress and Alexei.

The movement towards Catherine's autonomy is continued and its second stage concluded by an extraordinary scene in which it is Catherine herself who recedes from us, like the locket, into that sophisticated distance, too deep within herself for us to know her directly as we may know an innocent girl looking out at the world going by. Now the springs of her action can be her own and not imposed upon her. With much punctuating montage of people and bells (like those welcoming her to Russia and those ending the film) there is a baby (clearly Dmitri's) that the Empress is delighted by, Peter refuses congratulations on, Alexei is derided about, and Catherine is rewarded for. Like the scene at the wedding, what follows is a rendering of deepest consciousness which is laconic, enigmatic, withdrawn from us more than a little, yet utterly clear. There is no sympathy as in the cathedral and no witty sexuality as with the locket, but only, here at the very heart of the film, a totally private view of meditation, discovery of selfhood, understanding of one's relations to the world's possibilities and to one's own most inward sensibilities.

Catherine has had the baby and been rewarded; she lies in bed, again behind a curtain, as she receives the jewel which pays her (and parallels the locket she also received, used, and transcended; it will be itself succeeded by the bracelets she gives to the poor). We cut to a medium close-up as she twirls the jewel behind the gauze, looking pensive and thinking, one infers, how people use and discard others. She drops the jewel and Sternberg cuts to an extreme close-up not so much of Catherine (and thus unlike the cathedral close-up) but of the texture of the curtain, with Catherine's face behind seen almost more as planes and modellings of the gauze than as representation of herself. She turns her head one way as bells and crowds supervene for a moment and she thinks about them; then she turns her head back a little and the scene fades. Catherine is transformed into an enigmatic, objective, but completely expressive shape modelled within the gauze. The quality of her image fuses perfectly with the ironic and reflective, appraising and meditative but resentful and decisive character whose situation is to be almost obliterated within scurry and tumult but at the same time revealed, expressed, and articulated by the forceful and graceful design which the very pressure towards obscurity reveals.[12]

This moment of Catherine's privacy is not for our erotic contemplation but for our understanding of her consciousness. We see her act here, rejecting the jewel so contemptuous of her selfhood, reflecting on the context of crowds and public joy unconnected with her, and turning her head back to dismiss the sequence of which bells and crowds are a part. How she acts, what her consciousness is, should make it plain, as against Wood's claim, that what she does from here will not be to rejoin that world which has mistreated her. Adulthood is achieved in this scene; Catherine realizes she has to derive her strength from within rather than from anything laid on her from outside, whether by father or mother-in-law, by the promised idealism of love, or by public reward for public service. Catherine was manipulated and waiting at her wedding; she is simply herself here, in uttermost privacy, after having her child. She will herself do the manipulating the next time we see her in such a gauzy context.

A new stage begins, as the title card says, of Catherine's toughness, understanding, resilience; she starts to build her own life. She excludes Alexei and rejects the partisanship of Pimen the cleric, her independence reflected in her change of costume. It is a stage, of course, not just a sudden change. She has come far from silly little hoods, hoop skirts, and Gainsborough dresses, but has not yet reached the glories of the furry outfit she wears when choosing her soldier or of her final white mannish uniform. She holds the handkerchief that becomes her symbol; she manipulates it rather than being dominated by it as she tells Pimen she has stronger weapons than his politics and when she counters Peter's threats by spearing it on his sword in a wondrously witty exploitation of the fetish.

Then her challenge comes. The Empress dies and Peter asserts his power; but even while we see what looks like Catherine's quest for pleasure, we understand that there is a public dimension to her frivolity when she adds the army to her conquests. Catherine is completely masterful as she torments Alexei by mockingly putting a reminiscent straw in her mouth while she selects the magnificent Orlov from among the guardsmen and decorates Dmitri for the "bravery in action" that gave her a son. But that mastery is making itself felt in a transformation of hedonism into a more general satisfaction in the control of one's life, a transformation which culminates and is explicated in the scene of Alexei's rejection and Orlov's coming to her bed.

We think at first that now that Catherine has achieved virtual self-control she will simply take Alexei for herself at last. Alexei thinks so too, of course. She makes him say how he adores her, she entices him, she plays with the gauze curtain and she lies down invitingly, with the curtain in front of her so that Alexei, in bending over her, sweeps the curtain out beyond her head. It is at last as if he breaks through the veil that has been between Catherine and the world, but as that gauze removes itself from in front of Catherine, again something unexpected happens. She holds it loosely behind her and then for a moment pulls it taut, setting up a line in it as Alexei kisses her. Then she rises, with a little dismissing fillip of the curtain, and sets Alexei to blowing out the candles. It is the same little switch in tone as when instead of Catherine we saw the locket. After the emphasis on the devil shadow upon which the image of Alexei dissolves and which seems to imply that now Alexei is to be to Catherine what he was to the Empress, we almost expect a discreet fade to suggest Catherine has become the Empress in simple sexual freedom and unhindered gratification. The line in the gauze is a tension that can be resolved another way however. It is like the fingers on the guardsman's back, a kind of muscular sensual tensing, but it is different too. With the guardsman Catherine had dropped the locket and clutched the back, but here there is no dropping, rather a continuation of the same diversion of interest to the gauze as just before, still tantalizing but self-contained and controlled, not abandoned. It feels stylized, posed, externalized as before, but at the same time it also feels like something new: this time Catherine is not letting go in the way demonic Alexei's bending over and kissing her should allow.

The whole point is that Catherine is not submitting, but is at her most assertive. The tension line of the curtain is not muscular tension increasing sensualism but something left over, something to be done. What is left over is the moral which makes it quite right that Catherine lead Alexei through the scene she has been through before, having him blow out the candles and go for Orlov, not to revenge herself on Alexei so much as to demonstrate to him the falsity of the attitude that love is the private and final consolation in a bad world. Catherine lies cooly on her bed lightly touching the gauze that now neither conceals nor expresses her but simply is part of her whole life, while Alexei complies. It is a revenge, but a mild one given how unimportant sexual exclusivity comes to seem here; Catherine is not dehumanized to indulge it, nor does she become like the Empress—she is rather exactly different.

Alexei understands, as he says. They will "still be friends" as she asks, but his accommodation to the old ways has unsuited him for Catherine as she has become. He could have shared in Catherine's sense of clean, unmasochistic, sophisticated sexuality and self-expression, a sense utterly opposed to the barbarities of the Russian court with its glorious icons and paintings alternating with bare board walls, its opulence and its self-abasement, its brooding statues and its sense of everything being too big for people who try to get along in it and seem half crazy as they do so. There had been several times when he could have stood up for Catherine with the instinctive flair Orlov shows at the final dinner, but he did not. As Catherine sends him for Orlov she both pays him back for the personal betrayal and shows him how his chance has gone, how Orlov, with his diamonds and elegance, is the inheritor of what Alexei could have had. Alexei requests Orlov to carry to Catherine the message that he's taken the point, but stops—"No, don't tell her anything, she'll know"—and drops his head into shadow, not (as Wood argues) because Catherine has now become a part of the world she fought, but because she has become something different which he is debarred from joining. From here Alexei acts more as a narrator of Catherine's progress than as a factor in it.

In no sense, does Catherine replace Alexei with Orlov; she rejects Alexei and (without for a minute giving up sex or diamonds) stands on her own. The sensuality which was the first stage after submission is absorbed without sacrifice into a larger goal, as it always is in Sternberg's films. In *Jet Pilot* and *The Saga of Anatahan,* in *The Docks of New York, The Blue Angel,* and *The Devil is a Woman,* one sees that sex, while enormously important, is not all there is. There is a moral dimension to the adult personality which is called upon exactly at the point at which sexual satisfaction could, but should not, be taken as the ultimate good: assertion of one's sexuality becomes the type, not the alternative, of a generalized autonomy. Sternberg's films, often ironically but in *The Scarlet Empress* quite directly, present us with the coming to awareness, and usually to assertion, of that moral dimension.

From here, then, there is one long celebration of a new style of action and exhilaration to replace the brooding Russian craziness, from the banquet which balances the wedding banquet and in which Catherine finally ties her napkin to signify a very different bond from the one tied at the wedding, through to the end when the dove settles back on the post of the bell from which it had flown when Catherine selected Dmitri and thought she was becoming simply a hedonist. Orlov comes to Catherine's bed again but, instead of joining her, gives her his hand as she steps out fully dressed to lead her coup. Peter cowers fearfully when Orlov comes in and kills him, while Catherine becomes increasingly open and vital. The film becomes a montage of flags, drums, guns, icons, soldiers, and horses; and the screen surface itself seems more to render Catherine's tone than to encourage us to observe her personal reactions. Rather than private within the panoply, as at the wedding, she becomes public and absorbs it to herself, leading and symbolizing it but now fully part of it, not reserved or withdrawn or waiting at all. Through the anointing, the bell ringing, and the final ride up the stairs to the throne room, the quality is of the sudden freedom of action. We have seen submission squelched, alternatives denied, and a proper autonomy developed through abandon to feeling and then active control of the very feeling released by the abandon; at the end that feeling is released for everyone through Catherine's own release into the world of vigorous action.

There is just too much interplay here among character, theme, and image for us to think as Mulvey would have us, that an audience should respond (no matter how individual members may) with very simple pleasure in the image of Dietrich as the "ultimate fetish." Pleasure can and should come less from our look than from our thought occasioned by this film, thought about complex relations among submissiveness, shame, satisfaction, commitment, and assertiveness. Surprisingly, Wood's alternative reading not so much misses the film's point as denies it. For him, Catherine and Alexei were right for each other, and for Catherine to elect a less conventional sexuality and to let it be grounding but not purpose for a personal style full of vigor is in fact for her to become a " 'Messalina of the North.' " I am certain it is the basic point of the film to poke fun at just this idea.

If my reading has been convincing, then the interest that lies in the Wood and Mulvey errors should be clear. The story of a film does not have to matter much; one can think of cases, hardcore pornography, for instance, where such story as there is does not have the capacity to induce a viewer to consider its relationship to the visual pleasure the film offers. We have seen, however, that certain images of Dietrich in *The Scarlet Empress* have an important place in the story of the character she plays. That place prevents the images from "freez[ing] the flow of action in erotic contemplation" and encourages us to track the connotations of the images in all their fullness of intersection with the connotations of the story of which they are part. It is not a theoretical dictum but an empirical fact, if our reading is right, that story may matter for the way one should take the images, including taking them for the pleasure one should get from them. Since it may matter, then surely we should attend to the possibility of its mattering.

This is not to say that Mulvey is wrong to perceive in the image of Dietrich, in *The Scarlet Empress* as elsewhere, a quality of implausible and engrossing perfection which amounts to a distortion in the representation of a woman.[13] The distortion is in the direction of making her connote a quite unrealistic freedom from the challenges to sexuality which realistically-depicted women must be presumed to bring to any other realistically-depicted character and to the audience (of whatever sex). But that distortion plays against the connotation, suggested by the story of Catherine in its more realistic aspects, of ordinariness masked, hidden, withdrawn, reserved, but existent. Dietrich encourages being looked at as a sexual object, but in a film which also encourages her being looked at as a person whose status as sexual object is a developed stance, an instance of a persona with which a woman might respond to the problems and challenges of her world (itself a stylized, metaphoric version of a normal one).

The film considers fetishism rather than manipulating it. The Mulvey error was instructive, as promised. It encouraged us to realize that story and visual pleasure may have mutual influence on each other, that both are aspects of a film's implicational web, and that to give priority to one (for instance, the visual pleasure) risks being false to a film as a whole. It is the same with Wood's argument. The imagery has a dark side; not only is something important given up in any underplaying of straightforward romantic love but also callousness and coldness appear in the transformation of consciousness into action. One must attend to that undercutting quality of the imagery in a general accounting of the film, but surely not exclusively, not to the point of "abandon[ing] chronology." Despite Catherine's loss of intimacy and the imagery that suggests a progression to moral darkness, our evidence supports a reading that assents to what is positive in the triumphant Catherine. The fetishistic quality of Dietrich's image and the darkness of a certain strand of implication in the imagery exist. We would not wish them not to, for surely our general sense of a film's value comes not solely from its leading implication but from the rich presentation of the issues which bear on that implication, which qualify it and undercut it and make it worth thinking about. Sternberg films tend strongly to have that worth in their ongoing dialectic between tendencies toward the fixed and definable (on whatever side) and the sense of plenitude of implication with which the characters and the film itself round upon their schemata.

*University of Oregon*

## NOTES

[1] Robin Wood, "The Play of Light and Shade: *The Scarlet Empress*," *Film Comment*, 16 (March-April 1975), 6-12, rpt. in *Personal Views: Explorations in Film* (London: Gordon Fraser, 1976), pp. 94-113, to which my parenthetical citations refer.

Laura Mulvey, "Visual Pleasure and Narrative Cinema," *Screen,* 16 (Autumn 1975), 6-18, to which my citations refer, and rpt. in *Women and the Cinema,* ed. Karyn Kay and Gerald Peary (New York: Dutton, 1977), pp. 412-28. Mulvey takes Sternberg's films in general, though not *The Scarlet Empress* in particular, as exemplary of one of two principal varieties of visual pleasure in classic cinema (the other being Hitchcock's). Raymond Durgnat predates Wood's claim that, as he says, "Catherine's triumph is also a corruption," in "Six Films of Josef von Sternberg," first published under the pseudonym O. O. Green in *Movie,* 13 (1965), rpt. in *Movies and Methods,* ed. Bill Nichols (Berkeley: Univ. of California Press, 1976), p. 268. Joyce Rheuban, "Josef von Sternberg: The Scientist and the Vamp," *Sight and Sound,* 42 (Winter 1972/3), 34-40, like Wood and Durgnat, thinks Catherine becomes "a lascivious fiend" (p. 40), and that she represents one pole of the scientist/vamp, man/woman, concealment/revelation, "reason and control"/"dark forces" antinomy system in which Sternberg indulges. The thematic system has some truth to it, but misreadings of particular films make modification necessary. Andrew Sarris, *The Films of Josef von Sternberg* (New York: Museum of Modern Art, 1966), pp. 37-40, treats the good-temperedness of the progression to ecstasy as the leading quality, rightly minimizing the darker implications of which others make too much. Sarris misses, however, the level of quite serious (but not somber) implication deriving from Catherine's story.

[2] Note that the unraveling of the hermeneutic is not, quite apart from issues of theme, the only narrative pleasure. Northrop Frye, *Anatomy of Criticism* (Princeton, N.J.: Princeton Univ. Press, 1957), pp. 169-70, points out how comedy moves towards establishment not solution of a mystery, its movement being from *"pistis"* to *"gnosis,"* from "habit, ritual bondage, arbitrary law" to "a society controlled by youth and pragmatic freedom." It goes from "illusion to reality," where "illusion is whatever is fixed and definable," and reality is "whatever reality is, it's not *that.*" Sadistic voyeurism takes pleasure exactly in the inexorable revelation of something fixed and definable, the woman's inevitable guilt and its extension in the world's lack, a reality which is just what the comic movement opposes (and which is indeed, as we would expect, the goal and lesson of the opposite movement, the tragic).

[3] Monroe C. Beardsley, *Aesthetics: Problems in the Philosophy of Criticism* (New York: Harcourt, 1958). Beardsley's argument is grounding for my case in every respect. See also my "Human Experience and the Work Itself: A Review of Beardsley's *Aesthetics* for Film Critics," *Journal of the University Film Association,* 29 (Winter 1977), 25-32. To avoid confusion, I should specify that I mean by an aesthetic "philosophy of criticism, or *metacriticism*" (Beardsley, p. 4), roughly, the set of things it makes sense to say about aesthetic objects and the reasons the set makes sense.

[4] I thus extend Mulvey's "to-be-looked-at-ness" (p. 11) in line with her subsequent argument.

[5] On the open question of value, see Beardsley, p. 519. I label as the "open possibility" the case most sharply put with regard to the issue of understanding music (which is simply put as "hearing it fully"), p. 337.

[6] The relationship between the intent to deny the existence of aesthetic experience and hence aesthetic value and the argument from Moralism (of which Marxism is a variety), itself dependent on psychological definitions of value, is given concisely in Beardsley, pp. 564-65. On Marxism, see pp. 567-71. To refute psychological definitions is to refute Mulvey; what I attempt to make plausible here is that a particular film (e.g., *The Scarlet Empress*) can effect a response different in quality from the kind of pleasure Mulvey sees in it.

[7] F. C. Bartlett, *Remembering* (1932; rpt. Cambridge, Eng.: Cambridge Univ. Press, 1967), p. 206. On the "creative aspect of language use" see Noam Chomsky, *Cartesian Linguistics* (New York: Harper and Row, 1966).

[8] There are variations in the degree to which separation from the constricting world and independence in the satisfying world are achieved, from X-27's failure by both of her worlds to Immanuel Rath's failure of both of his. Catherine's is the most positive version in the canon.

[9] Sarris argues this (p. 39), as does Molly Haskell, *From Reverence to Rape* (New York: Holt, Rinehart, 1973), p. 109.

[10] To "make it new" was always Ezra Pound's advice. The "surprising turn" is what Arthur Koestler attributes, in organisms, to the principle of "bisociation," providing "originality" as against "habit," *The Act of Creation* (New York: Macmillan, 1964), esp. pp. 631, 659. For the notion of psychological theories as metaphoric rather

than literal bases for art and criticism, see my "Semiology, Human Nature, and John Ford," *Cinemonkey,* 5 (Spring 1979), 38-44.

[11] The image of the hand clutching the back has a charmingly dated quality when Sternberg uses it again as Anna kisses Shannon for the first time in *Jet Pilot,* a film with much the same story line as *The Scarlet Empress,* reaching through politics first to hedonism and then to a more general moral commitment.

[12] For defense of the notion that such fusion is plausible, see Beardsley, pp. 293-308.

[13] I do not use "distortion" pejoratively here, but in Beardsley's sense in which "distorted" is one of the possible contraries of "realistic." Others are "abstract," "idealized," and that quality in which something is not "realistic" if it does not "depict low life or the activities of the common man." Distortion is simply one dimension along which a representation can vary from realism. See Beardsley, pp. 285-88.

# Point of View and Narrative Voice in
## *The Grapes of Wrath:* Steinbeck and Ford

### DOUG EMORY

John Steinbeck's *The Grapes of Wrath* contains two distinct points of view: an apparently omniscient narrator who choşes to remain hidden and a much more overt narrator.[1] The former calls little attention to himself, allowing the characters to carry and interpret the action, while at the same time, providing the reader with large sections of landscape and character portraiture which focus attention on the story at hand. All of these portraits are characterized by the quality of stasis, the virtual stoppage of ongoing action that is typical of representation in the traditional pictorial mode.[2] The narrator of the interchapters, in contrast, directs attention to himself as historian, social critic, and philosopher. He breaks the illusion of reality present in the Joad family chapters and points out that the family's situation is but one illustration of a larger, potentially catastrophic social reality.

The narrator in these interchapters thus has much in common with pre-Flaubertian narrators because, in many cases, he interprets the action and creates an explicit narrative bias;[3] his point of view is less traditional in its rapid, plastic presentation of great amounts of space and in its impressionistic presentation of characters' minds as unmediated objects. Space in the interchapters becomes dynamic through the use of montage, and also through the sheer scope of the scenes which are presented. Alan Spiegel likens this narrative technique to the type of "additive montage" one commonly finds in Hollywood films.[4] Rather than first presenting two images which conflict (thesis and antithesis) in order to pave the way for a shot of the problem's resolution (synthesis) as did Eisenstein, the additive montage presents ideas and images which all build upon the feelings and themes expressed by the preceding images. Steinbeck's presentation of chapter 25 works in precisely this way. We are given rapidly shifting glimpses of tremendous waste which cause anger within us as readers, and these images portraying rage lead to the chapter's concluding editorial statement that, "in the souls of the people the grapes of wrath are filling and growing heavy, growing heavy for the vintage."[5] The narrative form of the additive literary montage aids Steinbeck's thematic content; and it places him squarely in the tradition of American writers of social protest as exemplified by many of his Depression-era contemporaries such as John dos Passos and James Agee.[6] The omniscient commentary, free entry into a character's mind, and additive montage help direct narrative judgments and editorials by providing the reader with a set historical and political perspective which shows the migrants' problems as issues which confront the nation as a whole. Whereas in the Joad family chapters, the reader is generally given a dramatic presentation of the story, in the interchapters there is often an intrusive voice which breaks off any ongoing narrative in order to interpret history or to philosophize, and which thus also suggests to the reader how to regard the situations that are being presented.[7]

The distinctions made about the twin narrators in Steinbeck's *The Grapes of Wrath* have not yet been applied to John Ford's version of the novel, for, until fairly recently, film was thought capable of only working within a single point of view.[8] Belief in the impersonal, objective nature of film dominated early critical theories; all films were commonly held to be narrated in the third person.[9] This idea of the omniscient, "anonymous 'grand image maker' "[10] was applied to the 1940 version of *The Grapes of Wrath,* and any aspects of that film which indicate a subjective narrative presence have consequently been ignored.[11] There are, to be sure, many examples of a single, objective point of view in the film. With only one exception, the movie follows the strict chronological flow of cause and effect which one expects in films with the continuity editing of the classical narrative cinema.[12] The film also presents its characters, for the most part, objectively: the film opens with "a long shot of a man (Tom Joad) coming over the horizon and walking down an Oklahoma country highway," and, while Tom remains fairly consistently present within the story space, we cannot in any way identify him as a guiding subjective consciousness because so many of the film's events occur without either his presence or his knowledge.[13] While the film does focus more completely on certain individuals (Tom, Casy, and Ma) than does the novel, it is still not dominated by any single individual who can be logically named as the narrative consciousness. A final way in which the film seems ostensibly based on the presentation of an omniscient, objective narrator is in the use of the invisible camera. The camera is, according to some critics, an objective medium in Ford's story, using montage, close-ups, or long shots only minimally, and demonstrating the Renaissance concept of perspective through a "preoccupation with straightforward, frontal, eye-level scenes."[14]

Focus on the film as objective has, at times, led to implicit disapproval. Critics quickly recognized that many of the events in the interchapters had been eliminated and found it very easy to claim that the revolutionary candor of these interchapters had also been eliminated.[15] The film itself was said to contain no explicit authorial commentary whatsoever.[16] Granted that Steinbeck's verbal narrative devices are eliminated from Ford's film, it does not necessarily follow that the film gives a strictly objective depiction. Actually, a series of visual motifs, along with several scenes which show us objects and events as the characters themselves see them, allow Ford to include a cinematic approximation of Steinbeck's more overt narrator. While one cannot definitely say that the film contains two distinct narrators, it is at least apparent that there are analogies to be drawn between the narrative bias in the film and that in the novel.[17] This subjective, indeed, nearly overt political stance of the film is best illustrated in three major sections: sequence 2, which shows the deserted Joad cabin; scene 9 of sequence 3, which shows

Ma Joad's reminiscences over a few of her possessions; and sequences 12 and 13, which show the Joad family's experiences at Hooverville and the Keene Ranch. These sections of the film can be seen to present motifs and concepts which recur throughout the film as a whole.

The most obviously subjective device in scene 6 of sequence 2 is the tale of dispossesion told by Muley himself. Muley opens by giving a generalized view of his situation and that of his neighbors: "The way it happened to me, a man come one day." The film, however, dissolves into a mindscreen,[18] a first-person series of images and in this sequence the viewer receives images biased in favor of Muley simply because he is the narrator of the tale: the image, for instance, of the confrontation between man and machine. The man who "come one day" arrives in an apparently new, beautiful car that stands in strict contrast to the poverty of Muley and his family. It is significant that the man never leaves his car but chooses to remain inside it, isolating himself as he evicts Muley and his family. Machinery is a visible threat again in Muley's memories of being tractored off his land. A montage sequence opens with a low angle shot of tractors dominating the entire screen. As the viewer is presented with the specific story of Muley's own eviction, the same camera angle is repeated. The viewer looks up at a tractor which looms threateningly over him and which is apparently being driven by some type of inhuman being (though this being is later revealed, as he removes his dust mask and goggles, to be the son of one of Muley's friends). This subjective camera perspective is maintained as Muley's house is destroyed. The camera watches, along with Muley and his family and from their point of view, as the tractor approaches the house. Throughout the film, this narrative use of machines will continue in much the same way. The viewer is shown the nearly human, ancient automobiles of the Okies (in a visual echo of the novel's statement that one character, Al Joad, "had become the soul of the car," p. 107) and then is forced to contrast these vehicles with those of the growers and the police. Every subsequent image we receive of these automobiles, though not governed by mindscreen, is colored by this early scene, a scene presented through Muley's subjective consciousness.

A second visual motif—light and shadow—is indicative of a subjectivity within the film and also begins during the deserted Joad cabin sequence. When Tom and Casy come upon Muley hiding in the darkness, Tom strikes a match to light Muley's face, the light making him appear haunted. This bizarre lighting effect is seen again through Muley's memory of an event. As the tractor rolls away after destroying Muley's farm, the viewer is given a high angle shot of three shadows cast on the ground—Muley, his wife, and his son—and the mindscreen ends with this shot. Before the mindscreen began, Muley had called himself a "graveyard ghost"; as the mindscreen passage itself ends, one sees this statement further supported by seeing that, within his mind, Muley considers himself as nothing more than a shadow. Another use of light (to become more prevalent in the Hooverville and Keene Ranch sequences) makes its first appearance soon after Muley's mindscreen ends. Threatening machinery again appears as a car comes over the hill, but the viewer sees only its headlights, and as those lights appear Muley exclaims, "That's them (the police)—them lights." He identifies the men with their searchlights, for the men themselves remain for the most part hidden in darkness behind those lights. The searchlights thus become hunting, threatening objects which are the instruments of a hidden evil; the light they cast serves to create a tension within the viewer, for the viewer, like the Okies, is given only a very limited view of whatever it is that guides those lights.

Subjective narrative devices again make themselves clearly evident during scene 9 of sequence 3. During this scene we receive an approximation of a character's visual viewpoint as Ma Joad sorts through a variety of her possessions. As Ma begins to go through her belongings, we see with her eyes, through subjective camera, the postcard from New York City, a newspaper clipping of Tom in jail, and a porcelain dog from the Saint Louis Exposition. When she holds her earrings to her ears, we see her in the mirror the same way she is seeing herself. A major difference between these shots and earlier near subjective shots is the inclusion on the soundtrack of the song, "The Red River Valley." This music cumulatively suggests "subjective sound (share my ears),"[19] for it is intimately associated with Ma throughout the movie. When it is next introduced she is dancing contentedly with Tom and her face reflects sentiment as well as nostalgia. Later the music is heard while Ma struggles to control her feelings as she and Tom part, probably for good. Excepting its presence under the opening title shot, the use of this song coincides exclusively with emotional moments in Ma's life and implies a presentation of her thoughts and feelings rather than those of an objective narrator.

The dramatic culmination of these narrative devices occurs during sequences 12 and 13 of the film. Both sequences include extremely powerful subjective camera shots, like that of the Joads' entry into Hooverville. In this lengthy shot the viewer drives through the poverty and waste of the camp with the Joads, seeing it all through the windshield of their truck. A little later, after the shooting of a woman, the viewer is presented with a brief point-of-view sequence. An old woman who is kneeling beside the wounded woman turns to look up at a deputy, and the next shot given is an extreme low-angle shot of the deputy seen through the old woman's eyes. The Joads' entrance to the Keene Ranch is marked by similar uses of the subjective camera. As they drive through the gate, a man steps out from the crowd and yells directly at the viewer, who is thus placed in the position of being a member of the entering line of migrant workers. More importantly, as Casy, who at times does seem to operate as a spokesman for the narrator, delivers his final speech to Tom, he appears to us through Tom's eyes. The camera presents a low-angle shot of him, and, as he leans forward toward Tom, he accordingly leans forward toward the camera, or our eyes as viewers, and comes to dominate the entire screen. This serves to present Casy in very much the sense that he appears to Tom by the film's end. The use of the subjective camera in this sequence, along with the haunting lighting effects, serves to transform Casy into an otherworldly, larger-than-life figure—a Christlike figure haloed by light and placed high above us in the space of the scene.

Placement and the use of light and dark also are used to create a subjective point of view in scenes 30 and 36 through 41. Grid figures which seem to capture the characters within a stark geometric shape are repeated in shots through car windows, windshields, a chain link fence, and doorways; but more noticeable for the purpose of the building of tension is the continual use of characters (generally "tin star men") who are only partially seen because of the darkness and "the arbitrary cutting-off performed by the frame."[20] When the Joads leave Hooverville and are stopped by a mob, for example, a shadow blackens half the screen as Tom is confronted at the driver's side of the truck. Tom's face is fully illuminated by a flashlight, but the man holding it is unseen and is unnaturally severed in turn by the restrictions imposed by the frame. This type of shot is repeated several times throughout the Keene Ranch sequence, and each time a sense of surprise and uneasiness is created as a man suddenly interjects himself onto the screen but never allows himself to be completely perceived by the viewer. That these faceless men often carry flashlights and shine those lights directly into the eyes of the interrogated is the continuation of the searchlight-shadow motif first seen at the end of sequence 2.

The number of times this visual motif is repeated (and the fact that each time it is, a threat presents itself within the narrative) makes the motif extremely noticeable: agricultural inspectors shine a flashlight on dead Granma Joad; the mob that stops the family outside Hooverville shines a light on Tom; a guard at the Keene Ranch does the same when Tom begins to go for a walk; and just before Tom leaves the government camp, a policeman shines a light into the Joad tent. These are only a few of the available examples. The most powerful use of this motif, of course, occurs during Casy's death scene. Several unseen men on a bridge suddenly focus their flashlights on Tom and Casy while remaining unilluminated themselves even during the fight. Thus Casy appears to be killed by a shadow rather than a man. Both the framing and the use of shadows present the viewer with the idea of a covert evil. The people who are exploiting and injuring the Okies are constantly left hidden by their placement within the frame or by the use of lighting effects. The repetition of these images creates a subjective response and certain ideologic perceptions within the spectator. Because of this, the narrative placement of the "spectator in the text" serves as a revelation of and factor in the creation of the film's moral views.[21]

Mindscreen, music, lighting, and framing, then, stand as clear indications that there is a greater degree of subjectivity and subsequent narrative bias in Ford's *The Grapes of Wrath* than has commonly been supposed. Even though the continuity of the plot is never truly disrupted for editorial purposes, it is apparent that the revolutionary fervor one finds in Steinbeck's novel has not been eliminated; instead there has only been a change in the narrative devices used to suggest much the same political and economic evil. The degree of difference in Steinbeck's and Ford's representations can be seen by comparing the images in Steinbeck's final revolutionary interchapter and the final image in Ford's film. While Steinbeck's work speaks of the sheriff's ordering rifles and swearing in deputies to fight off the masses of starving people, and talks of the wrath growing inside those people, Ford's film ends with a shot of a line of trucks passing behind an almost hidden, innocuous sign on which, in ironic contrast to Ma's final optimistic statement, is printed the word "Danger." While one could speculate as to whether or not the Hollywood production system forced Ford to present his view of the conflict more subtly than did Steinbeck, it still remains obvious that, while he did not utilize Steinbeck's two demonstrably different narrators within his film, he did create a narrative voice analogous to the voice in Steinbeck's interchapters capable of a highly subjective presentation of a political situation as well as an objective one.

*Arizona State University*

## NOTES

[1] See, for example, Peter Lisca's *The Wide World of John Steinbeck* (New Brunswick, N.J.: Rutgers Univ. Press, 1958), pp. 154-60.

[2] Sean Shesgreen, *Literary Portraits in the Novels of Henry Fielding* (DeKalb: Northern Illinois Univ. Press, 1972), p. 39.

[3] See Russell Campbell, "Trampling Out the Vintage: Sour Grapes," in *The Modern American Novel and the Movies,* ed. Gerald Peary and Roger Shatzkin (New York: Ungar, 1978), pp. 110-12.

[4] Alan Spiegel, *Fiction and the Camera Eye: Visual Consciousness in Film and the Modern Novel* (Charlottesville: Univ. Press of Virginia, 1976), p. 179.

[5] John Steinbeck, *The Grapes of Wrath* (New York: Viking, 1966), p. 311. All further references to this work appear in the text.

[6] Spiegel, p. 179.

[7] The philosophic and symbolic aspects of the narrator's statements have been analyzed in greater depth than have the technical elements which constitute the narrative voice and point of view; see, for instance, Joseph Fontenrose, *John Steinbeck: An Introduction and Interpretation* (New York: Holt, Rinehart, 1963).

[8] The classical narrative cinema is generally characterized by a seamless narrative and unified, objective point of view. Recent critical articles which have begun analyzing the subjective aspects of Ford's work include Nick Browne, "The Spectator-in-the-Text: The Rhetoric of *Stagecoach,"* in *Film Quarterly,* 29 (Winter 1975-76), 26-38; William Luhr and Peter Lehman, *Authorship and Narrative in the Cinema* (New York: G. P. Putnam's Sons, 1977); Lehman, "An Absence Which Becomes a Legendary Presence: John Ford's Structured Use of Off-Screen Space," *Wide Angle,* 2, No. 4 (1978), 36-42; and Douglas Gomery, "Mise-en-scène in John Ford's *My Darling Clementine,"* *Wide Angle,* 2, No. 4 (1978), 15-19.

[9] Bruce Kawin, *Mindscreen: Bergman, Godard, and First-Person Film* (Princeton, N.J.: Princeton Univ. Press, 1978), p. 4: "The 'impersonal' nature of photography, for instance, appears to have dominated many of our rhetorical assumptions, so that a wide range of film theorists generally accept that a film must be narrated in the third person . . . ."

[10] Kawin, p. 18.

[11] Warren French, *Filmguide to "The Grapes of Wrath"* (Bloomington: Indiana Univ. Press, 1973), George Bluestone, *Novels into Film* (1957; rpt. Berkeley: Univ. of California Press, 1968), and Campbell focus for the most part on the apparent changes in narrative bias occasioned by the film's adaptation of the novel's plot.

[12] For a discussion of narrative forms and their applications in the classical narrative cinema, see David Bordwell and Kristin Thompson's *Film Art: An Introduction* (Reading, Mass.: Addison-Wesley, 1979), pp. 47-72.

[13] French, p. 3. I follow French's sequence and scene division throughout.

[14] French, p. 33.

[15] Campbell, French, and Bluestone make statements to this effect, and the Feb. 12, 1940 issue of *Time* praised the film for purging the "propaganda and phony pathos"

of "the editorial rash that blotched the Steinbeck book."

[16] Bluestone, pp. 162-63.

[17] Peter Lehman, in his *Wide Angle* article cited above (p. 36), states that there is a need for analysis and recognition of the ideologic consequences of Ford's style; such a recognition becomes especially important in understanding an adaptation of so politically inspired a work as *The Grapes of Wrath*.

[18] Kawin defines mindscreen as a type of first-person narration in which we share a character's thoughts. We accordingly see images from the character's subjective perspective, as he/she perceives them. I follow Kawin's terminology of mindscreen, subjective camera, and subjective sound.

[19] Kawin, p. 190.

[20] Seymour Chatman, *Story and Discourse: Narrative Structure in Fiction and Film* (Ithaca, N.Y.: Cornell Univ. Press, 1978), p. 96. The concept of framing as a statement of the narrative voice has been discussed at length in the Browne article cited above. Browne argues convincingly that framing in *Stagecoach* is directed toward the "spectator in the text," a cinematic version of Wayne C. Booth's implied reader, and is intended as a type of editorial statement supplying the narrator's moral commentary. Much the same device seems to be at work throughout portions of *The Grapes of Wrath*. For a concise discussion of the spectator's place within the text, see Robert T. Eberwein, "Spectator-Viewer," in *Wide Angle,* 2, No. 2 (1978), 4-9.

[21] Browne, p. 35. Browne's analysis of *Stagecoach* again applies very well here.

# Notes on Contributors

**Dudley Andrew** is a Professor of Communication and Theater Arts and of Comparative Literature at the University of Iowa. He has written many articles as well as *The Major Film Theories* (1976); *André Bazin* (1978); and the forthcoming *Kenji Mizoguchi: A Guide to References and Resources*. He is presently researching the history of French film from 1930 to 1970 and planning a second book on film theory.

**William Cadbury**, Professor of Film Studies at the University of Oregon who has published widely in literary periodicals, has more recently turned to film studies: an essay on André Bazin for *Journal of Modern Literature,* an article on Griffith's *Intolerance* for *Film Quarterly,* and separate essays on Auteurism and on John Ford for *Cinemonkey.* He has just coauthored a book-length manuscript entitled "Counter Theory: Problems in the Philosophy of Film Criticism."

**Joan Dagle** is a member of the Film Studies faculty and an Assistant Professor of English at Rhode Island College. She has an article on Boris Uspensky's *A Poetics of Composition* in NOVEL and is at work on studies of Alfred Hitchcock and "The Poetics of Omniscience and the English Novel."

**Doug Emory** is a Teaching Associate and a doctoral candidate at Arizona State University, where he is continuing research on Steinbeck and other American writers of the Depression era.

**Barry Keith Grant** is an Assistant Professor of Film and Popular Culture at Brock University, St. Catharines, Ontario. He has authored essays on film genre and has edited the anthology, *Film Genre: Theory and Criticism* (1977). Other publications include an article on auteur criticism for *Sphinx,* one on style for *Canadian Review of American Studies,* and one on Whitman and Eisenstein for *Literature/Film Quarterly.* He is completing a book on film genre and an anthology on teaching film.

**Michael Klein**, an Assistant Professor at Rutgers University, has written on François Truffaut for the anthology *Film And/As Literature* (1978) and has edited and contributed to *The English Novel and the Movies* (1980). He is writing a book-length manuscript entitled "Words and Images: The Novels, Scripts and Films of F. Scott Fitzgerald." Recently he completed a cinematic novel.

**Judith Mayne** is an Assistant Professor of French at The Ohio State University. Her most recent publications include an article on *Hiroshima mon amour* and a study of women in Soviet Cinema of the 1920s. She is working on a book on private and public space in film narrative.

**Peter Ruppert**, an Associate Professor at Florida State University, has had articles on Max Frisch appear in *Biography* and *Monatshefte*, on Jean-Paul Sartre and Rainier Maria Rilke in *Comparative Literature,* and on Utopian thinking in the *Southern Humanities Review.* He has just edited *Ideas of Order in Literature and Film* (1981) and is now writing a book about Utopian literature.

**Robert T. Self** is an Associate Professor of English at Northern Illinois University where he teaches American literature and film. He is the author of *Barrett Wendell* (1975), the editor of *Literature, Politics, and Society: The Collected Essays of Barrett Wendell* (1977), and has published film studies in *Style, Journal of Popular Film* and *Film Criticism.* Research in progress includes a study of the film career of Robert Altman.

**Ulrich Wicks**, Associate Professor of English at the University of Maine at Orono, has published numerous articles on picaresque narratives and "Literature/Film: A Bibliography" for *Literature/Film Quarterly.* He is continuing research on picaresque fiction and on self-reflexivity in addition to studying point of view in narrative film and fiction.

# Editors' Note

The editors would like to thank all those people who took time away from their own tasks to read and evaluate manuscripts: Kenneth D. Alley, Norman A. Anderson, Jay R. Balderson, Arnold E. Chandler, Jerome Delamater, Thomas P. Joswick, Charles W. Mayer, William R. Risley, Rulon Smithson, Margene Weiss.